Helen McKenzie

UTTERLY BRITISH MAPS

An atlas of Britain's quirks and quibbles

National Trust

Published by National Trust Books
An imprint of HarperCollins Publishers
1 London Bridge Street,
London SE1 9GF
www.harpercollins.co.uk

HarperCollins Publishers
Macken House, 39/40 Mayor Street Upper,
Dublin 1, D01 C9W8, Ireland

First published 2025
© National Trust Books 2025
Text and maps © Helen McKenzie 2025

ISBN 978-0-00-873676-7
10 9 8 7 6 5 4 3 2 1

All rights reserved. No part of this publication may be reproduced, stored in a retrieval system, or transmitted, in any form or by any means, electronic, mechanical, photocopying, recording or otherwise without the prior permission in writing of the publisher and copyright owners.

Without limiting the exclusive rights of any author, contributor or the publisher of this publication, any unauthorised use of this publication to train generative artificial intelligence (AI) technologies is expressly prohibited. HarperCollins also exercise their rights under Article 4(3) of the Digital Single Market Directive 2019/790 and expressly reserve this publication from the text and data mining exception.

The contents of this publication are believed correct at the time of printing. Nevertheless, the publisher can accept no responsibility for errors or omissions, changes in the detail given or for any expense or loss thereby caused.

A catalogue record for this book is available from the British Library.

Printed and bound in India by Replika Press Pvt. Ltd.

If you would like to comment on any aspect of this book, please contact us at the above address or national.trust@harpercollins.co.uk

National Trust publications are available at National Trust shops or online at nationaltrustbooks.co.uk

MIX
Paper | Supporting responsible forestry
FSC
www.fsc.org
FSC™ C007454

This book contains FSC™ certified paper and other controlled sources to ensure responsible forest management.

For more information visit: www.harpercollins.co.uk/green

Contents

Note on the Maps	5
Place	7
Heritage & History	29
Food & Drink	45
Plants & Animals	65
Weather	85
Transport	101
Lifestyle & Hobbies	117
Index	132
Acknowledgements	134

Definitions

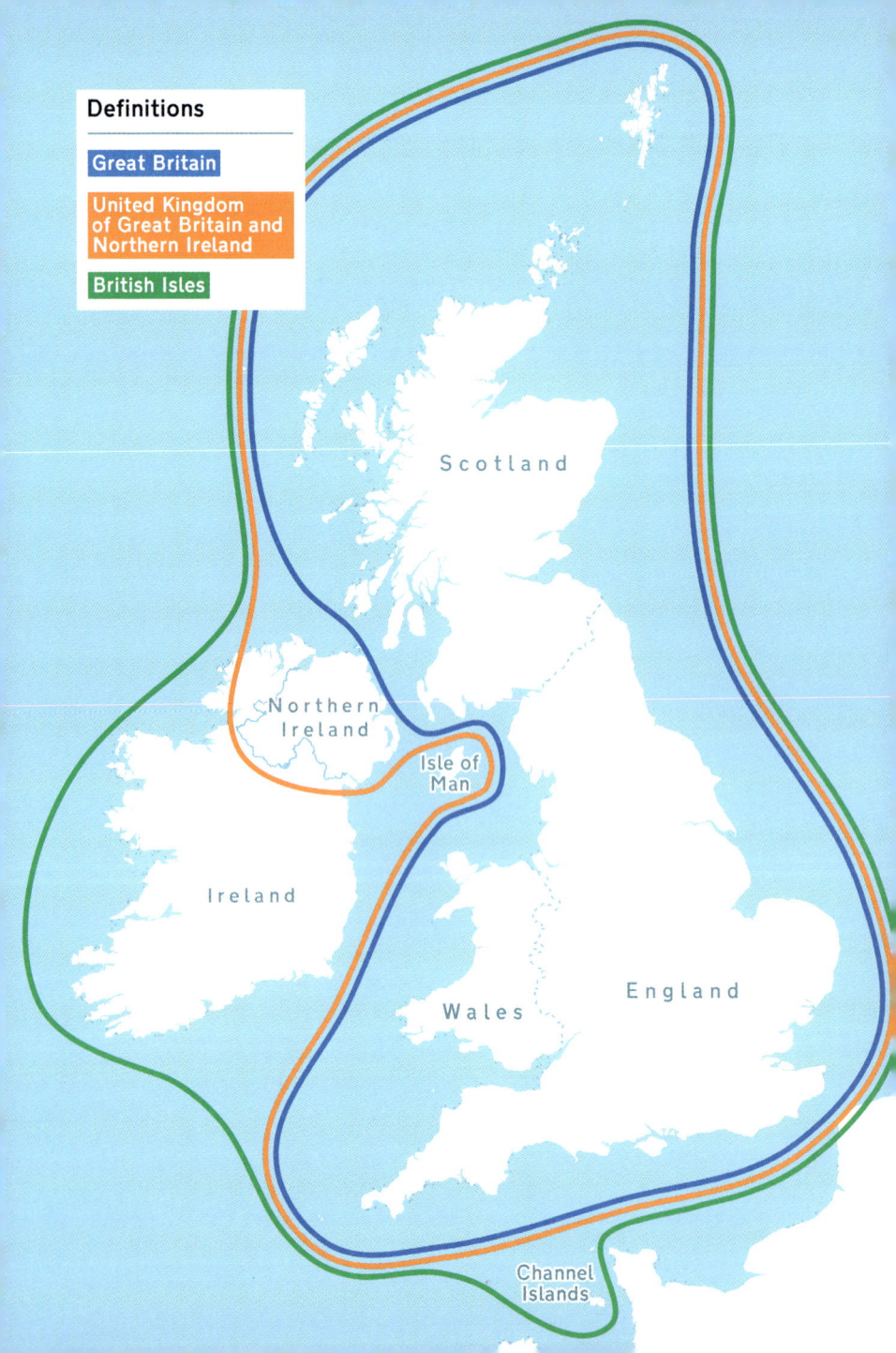

- Great Britain
- United Kingdom of Great Britain and Northern Ireland
- British Isles

Scotland

Northern Ireland

Isle of Man

Ireland

Wales

England

Channel Islands

Note on the maps

All of the maps in this book are original creations. It would not have been possible to make them without the fantastic culture of open data that exists in the UK. A full list of sources for the maps can be found at the end of this book.

In addition, thanks must be given to those who enthusiastically took part in the 'Utterly British Maps' survey which was commissioned for this book to help capture and map the unique concept of 'Britishness'.

What is the UK?

Mapping this country is more complicated than most – in part because we're kind of one country, but we're also kind of four countries ... and then a few other bits too.

So, let's start like all good things should – with a geography lesson. First, we have 'Great Britain'. This consists of England, Wales and Scotland. Add Northern Ireland to that, and you have the 'United Kingdom of Great Britain and Northern Ireland' (the UK, for short). Then, you have the 'British Isles'. This is the UK, the Isle of Man, the Channel Islands and Ireland.

Unnecessarily confusing? Bafflingly complicated? Welcome to Britain ... or do I mean the UK? Either way, in this book we'll be mostly concerned with mapping the UK – that is, the orange bit of this map.

Place

From Upton Snodsbury to
Cucumber Corner – uncovering the
UK's story through place

Weird place names

Of the many things that make Britain great, surely our weird and wonderful place names have to be up there.

Many of these are just fantastically mundane: Hose, Jump and Droop are great examples, although surely Dull wins the award for the most brilliantly boring place name. Others are more eccentric, like Cucumber Corner, Crackpot and Bishop's Itchington.

There are some places where someone has clearly just turned up and named a town after themselves in the most low-effort way; Ianstown and Keith, we're looking at you. On the other hand, there are places that just make you wonder how they ended up with their name. For instance ... what on earth happened in Pity Me?

Then there are the place names on the ruder side. If you know where to look, you'll find some incredibly rude place names across the UK ... but this is a family friendly book, so we'll stop at Scratchy Bottom.

And, speaking of Bottoms ...

Ianstown
Keith
Lost
Dull
California
Bonkle
Rotten Bottom
Once Brewed
No Place
Pity Me
Stranagalwilly
Leggs
Nutt's Corner
Crackpot
Giggleswick
Blubberhouses
Ramsbottom
Jump
Vulcan Village
Over Peover
Hugmore
Great Snoring
Cucumber Corner
Hose
Bunny
Sheepy Parva
Barton in the Beans
Plwmp
Upton Snodsbury
Bishop's Itchington
Matching Tye
Splott
Nether Wallop
Great Bottom Flash
Camel
Curry Mallet
Droop
Beer
Scratchy Bottom
Flushing

Bottoms of Britain

Did you know there are nearly 400 places in the UK with 'bottom' in their name? These include the Lancashire town of Ramsbottom, with a population of over 17,000, the wooded valley of Betty Mundy's Bottom in Hampshire and the Sussex ridge of Loose Bottom, which boasts – despite the name – spectacular views. In the UK, you simply can't move without bumping into bottoms.

You can explore all of these in this map, with some of our favourites labelled for your enjoyment.

So, what's behind this craze? Well, etymologically speaking, the place name 'bottom' derives from the Old English for 'broad river valley' or 'valley floor'. This may be why British bottoms are almost entirely found in England. They are particularly common in the lowland stretch between the Peak District and the Yorkshire Dales, the New Forest and the valleys of the Chilterns – the 'bottoms' of surrounding upland areas, if you will.

Greenbottom

Bottoms

- Top Bottoms
- Other Bottoms

Pinksey Bottom
Hole Bottom
Ramsbottom
Bottom o'th'Moor
Bottom Boat
Broadbottom
Muckton Bottom
Six Mile Bottom
Watery Bottom
Dry Bottom
Hogpits Bottom
Deans Bottom
Kent's Bottom
Great Bottom Flash
Pett Bottom
Loose Bottom
Fishpond Bottom
Betty Mundy's Bottom
Puddington Bottom
Happy Bottom
Breaky Bottom
Scratchy Bottom

Location	Nickname
Shetland Islands	**Absent Isles**
Barra	**Barradise**
Inverness	**The Sneck**
Aberdeen	**Furry Boots**
Dundee	**Fundee**
Edinburgh	**Auld Reekie**
Newcastle upon Tyne	**The Toon**
Belfast	**Old Smoke**
Pontefract	**Ponte Carlo**
Scarborough	**Scarbados**
Wakefield	**Shakey Wakey**
Salford	**Costa del Salford**
Derby	**Derbados**
Skegness	**Skeggy**
Stoke-on-Trent	**The Potteries**
Loughborough	**Loogabarooga**
Leicester	**City of Kings**
Cambridge	**Silicon Fen**
Biggleswade	**Biggleswiggle**
Ipswich	**Hipswic**
Swansea	**Copperopolis**
Newport	**Zooport**
Basingstoke	**Amazingstoke**
Barry	**Barrybados**
Chippenham	**Chips and Ham**
Canterbury	**Banterbury**
Weston-super-Mare	**Weston-super-Mud**
Padstow	**Padstein**
St Austell	**Snozzle**
Torbay	**Torbados**
Hove	**Hove, Actually**
Plymouth	**Guzz**

Town nicknames

Renowned around the world for our baffling place names (looking for Barrow Gurney? It's just down the road from Chew Magna and Publow), we Brits like to make things even more interesting by giving charming (or sometimes not so charming) nicknames to our beloved towns and cities.

Some of these are simply shortened versions of their 'official' names – for instance Doncaster, Skegness and Scunthorpe are often referred to as 'Donny', 'Skeggy' and 'Scunny' respectively. Other nicknames relate to industry – for example, Swansea being donned 'Copperopolis' – or history, with Leicester being nicknamed 'City of Kings' after the remains of Richard III were found in a car park.

Never ones to miss an opportunity for irony, we also often give nicknames which allude to sunnier and – dare I say it – slightly more glamorous climes. Ponte Carlo (Pontefract), Costa del Salford (Salford), Lich Vegas (Lichfield) and Barrybados (Barry) are all great examples of us at our sarcastic best.

Britain's history in 12 place names

While place names of the UK are often incredibly amusing, they are also incredibly interesting tools to help tell the story of how Britain has evolved over time.

From the Normans, Saxons, Vikings, Romans and all the way back to the native Britons, the UK has been influenced by a wide range of cultures throughout our history – a story that is told in our place names.

For example, forms originating in Roman Latin – such as -caster and -cester – are more common across England, reflecting the extent of the Roman Empire. Forms derived from Old English – like -borough, -wich and -stead – often have a similar geography. Old Norse forms like -thorpe are more likely to be found in the north-east of England across the once Danish-ruled Danelaw. Similarly, Welsh, Scots Gaelic, Irish, Cumbric and Cornish forms are most common in these exact places.

You can explore the density of some of these place name forms – and their origins and meanings – across the next few pages.

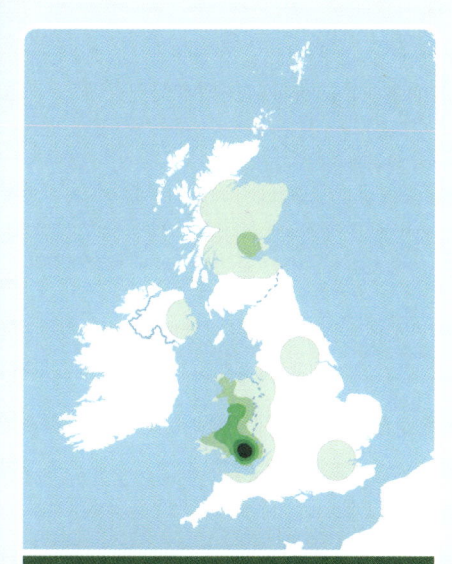

Aber-
Cornish, Cumbric, Pictish, Welsh: river mouth or meeting

Bal-
Scots Gaelic, Irish: farm, homestead or mouth, approach

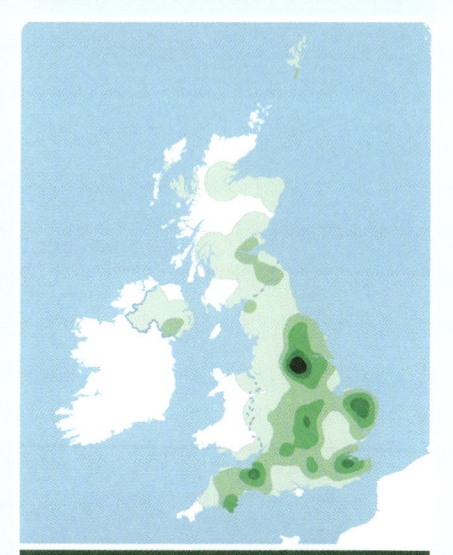

-borough, -burgh, -brough, -brugh
Old English: fortified enclosure

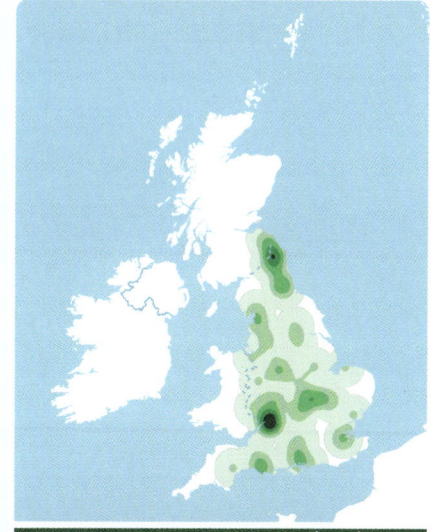

-caster, -cester, -chester, -(c/x)eter
Old English, Latin: camp or fortification

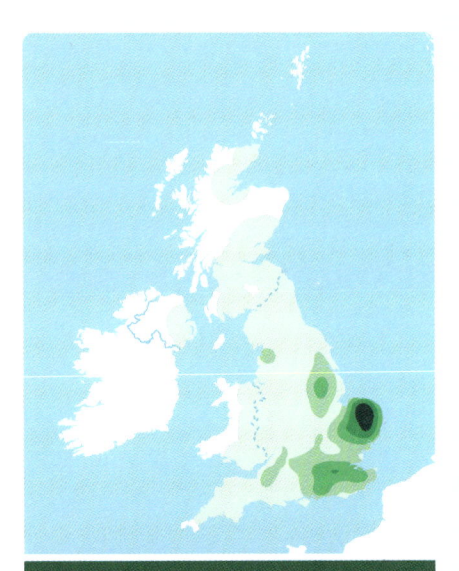

-ham
Old English: farm, homestead

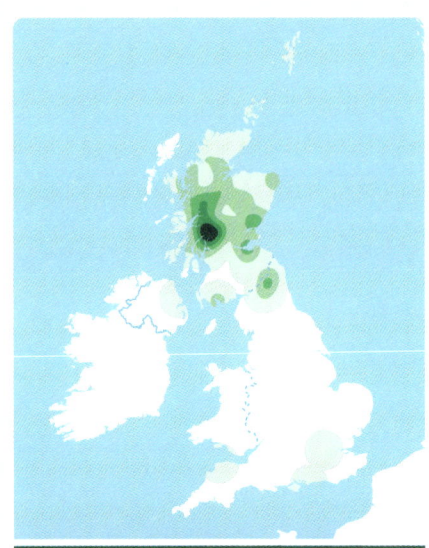

Inver-, Inner-
Scots Gaelic: river mouth or confluence

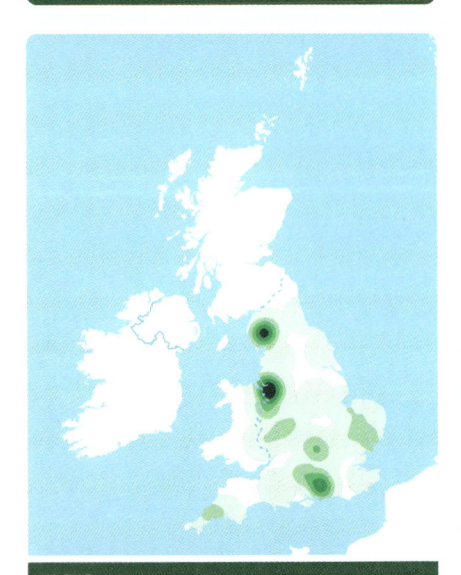

-mere
Old English: lake, pool

-ness
Old English, Old Norse: promontory, headland

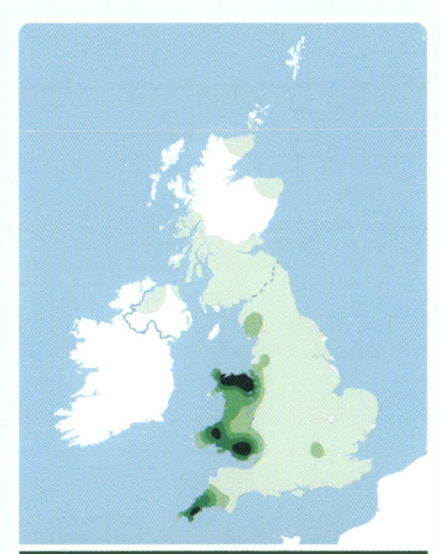

Pen-, Pedn-
Cornish, Cumbric, Pictish, Welsh: head, headland, top, end of

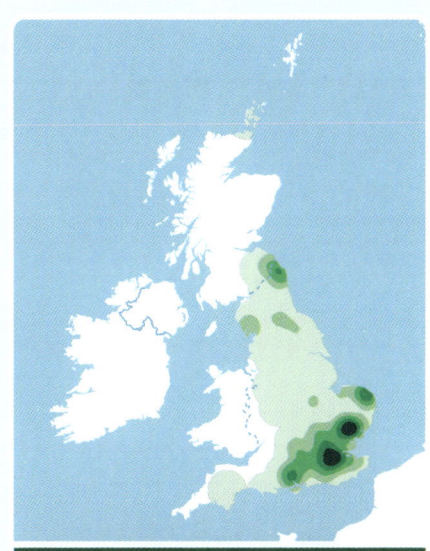

-stead
Old English: place, enclosed pasture

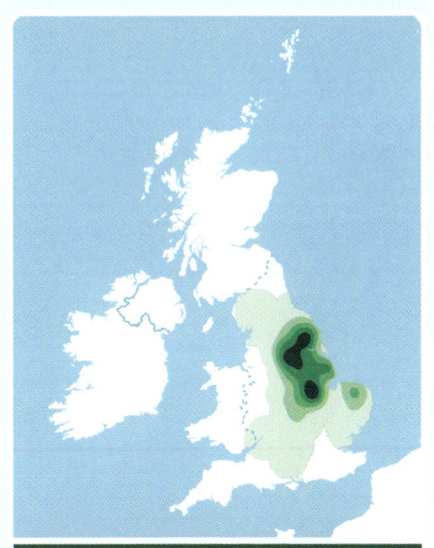

-thorp, -thorpe
Old Norse: secondary settlement

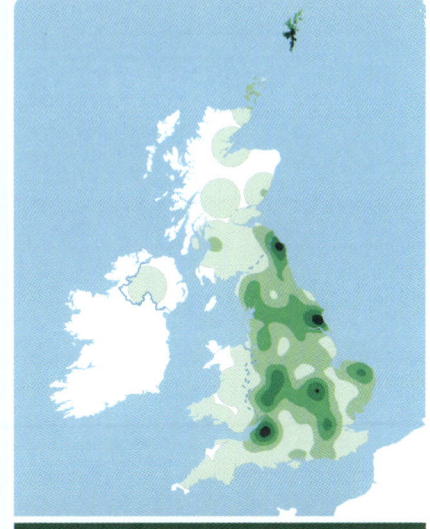

-wick, -wich, -wyke, -wych
Old English, Latin: place, settlement

A world of twin towns

Whenever you drive into a town, you'll often see 'Twinned with ...' cheerfully emblazoned on the welcome sign. But did you ever wonder why? Don't worry, we've got the twinned town facts to make you a legend at your next pub quiz.

The concept of 'twinning' began during the Second World War and was designed to promote cultural and commercial links between towns in different countries. There are roughly 1,600 cities, towns and villages around the world which have the honour – nay, the privilege – of being twinned with some of our most illustrious towns. These 'twinnings' range from the more geographically intimate pairing of Calais and Dover (just 26.7 miles/43km apart) to the most long-distance twinning: the Christchurches of New Zealand and Dorset, separated by nearly 12,400 miles (20,000km).

Speaking of Dorset, there must be something in the water there. While most towns are content with one – maybe two – pairings, Sherborne holds the twinned town record with 35! Perhaps this is because they're a member of the European Union's 'Douzelage' – a town twinning association – or perhaps they're just super friendly.

And what about who we're twinning with? Well, we seem to be most keen on our friends in Europe. A whopping 562 of our twins are in France, followed by 372 in Germany, and 122 in the USA.

Lighthouse locations and ranges

Just like piers, fish and chips and dive-bombing seagulls, our coastline wouldn't feel complete without lighthouses. Often overlooking dramatic clifftops or standing guard over historic harbours, lighthouses are an iconic and nostalgic sight.

The UK's coastline features around 210 active lighthouses, meaning there is one lighthouse for every 37 miles (60km) of coastline. They aren't evenly distributed, however. More lighthouses can be found around particularly hazardous parts of the coastline, such as around Orkney, the Shetland Islands and Lizard Point – the southernmost point of the UK.

Lighthouses have a long and storied history. The oldest active lighthouse is the Isle of Wight's Needles Lighthouse. Originally built in 1785 – and rebuilt in 1859 – it has served as a beacon guiding ships up the narrow and rocky Solent for over 200 years. They have also frequently been locations of scientific and technological innovation. The South Foreland Lighthouse in Dover, Kent, was the first lighthouse to use an electric light and was used by Guglielmo Marconi in his pioneering work on wireless radio transmissions.

In addition to these active lighthouses, many inactive ones still line our coast – preserved for their great history, sense of nostalgia and crucial family-photo backdrop. The oldest of these is St Catherine's Oratory (known affectionately as the Pepperpot). Looking out from one of the highest parts of the Isle of Wight, it dates back to 1328, making it the only standing medieval lighthouse.

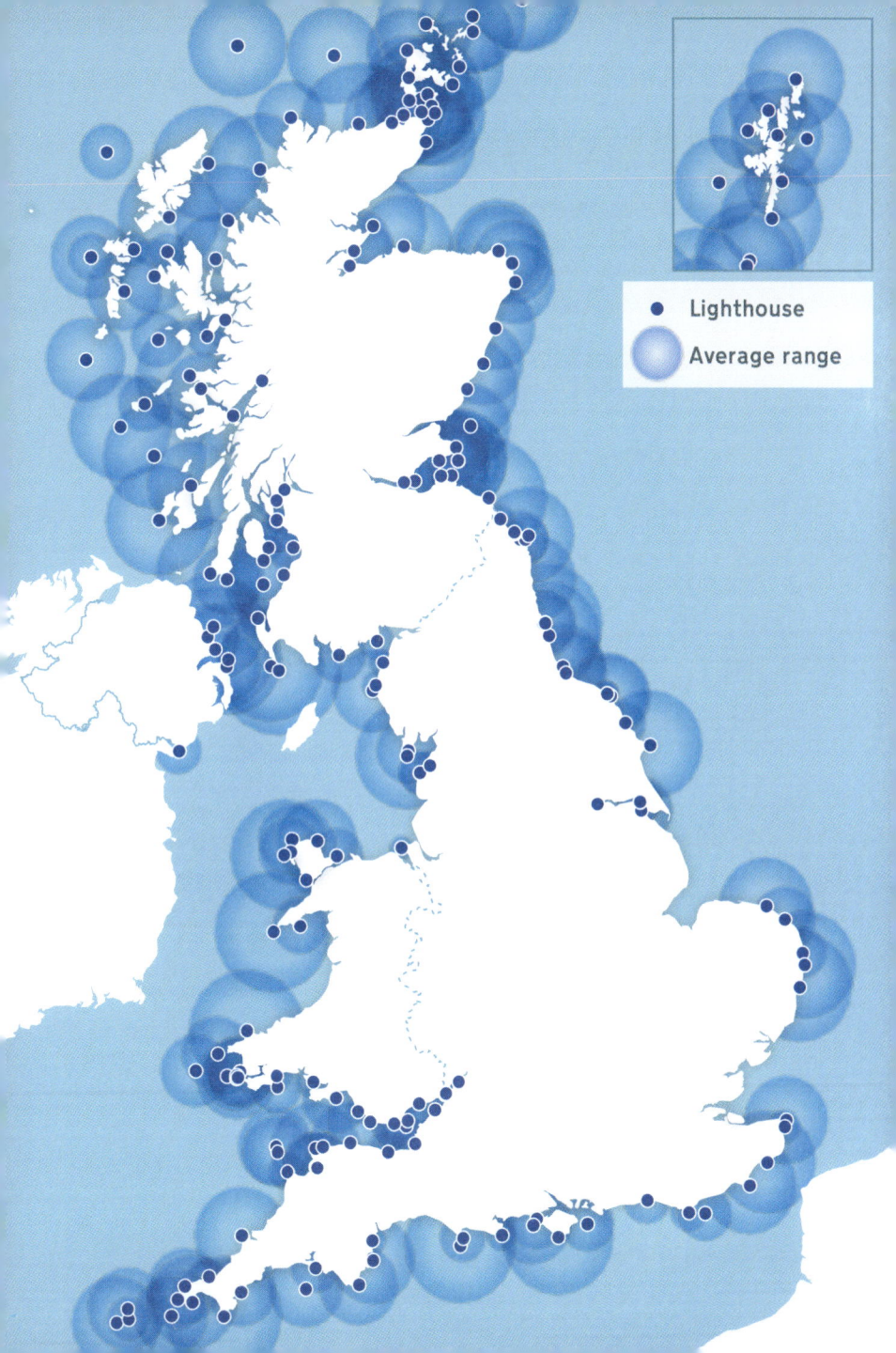

- Lighthouse
- Average range

Longest seaside piers

There's something about seaside pleasure piers. They evoke a nostalgia for a simpler time – a time of promenades, Punch and Judy and those fantastic 'sea bathing' costumes which really are due a comeback.

A mainstay of the Victorian era, the first pleasure pier is the still-standing Ryde Pier on the Isle of Wight, which was built in 1814, predominantly as a means of easily transporting passengers from shore to ship. Soon, the popularity of piers exploded, and at one point there were over 100 piers dotted around the British coastline.

However, today only 46 remain – mostly in England and Wales.

Southend Pier, stretching a massive 2,140m (7,019ft or 1.33 miles), is the longest pleasure pier in the world. It's so enormous that it even has its own railway line!

At the other end of the scale is the diminutive Clarence Pier in Portsmouth, measuring in at a petite 62 metres. There are also a host of 'officially unrecognised' piers, owing to their size – such as Burnham-on-Sea's minute 37-metre pier – or location, like Gravesend's Royal Terrace which is actually on a river.

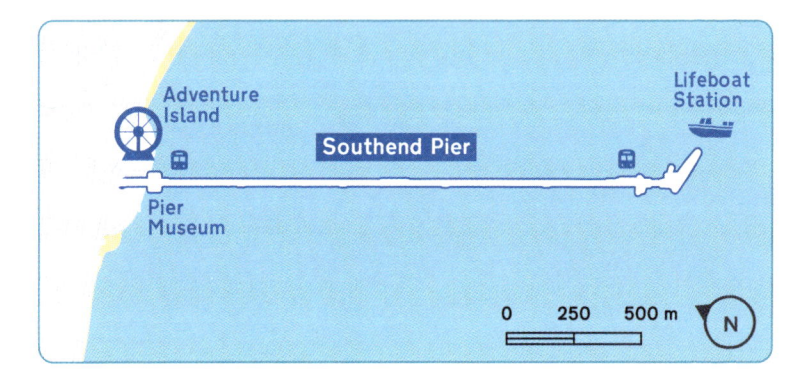

Shortest Pier • **Longest Pier**

- Llandudno: 765m
- Southport: 1,179m
- Garth: 503m
- South Pier, Lowestoft: 440m
- Walton: 870m
- Southend: 2,140m
- Clarence Pier: 62m
- Hythe: 700m
- Folkestone: 533m
- Palace Pier, Brighton: 574m
- Ryde: 745m

Foula

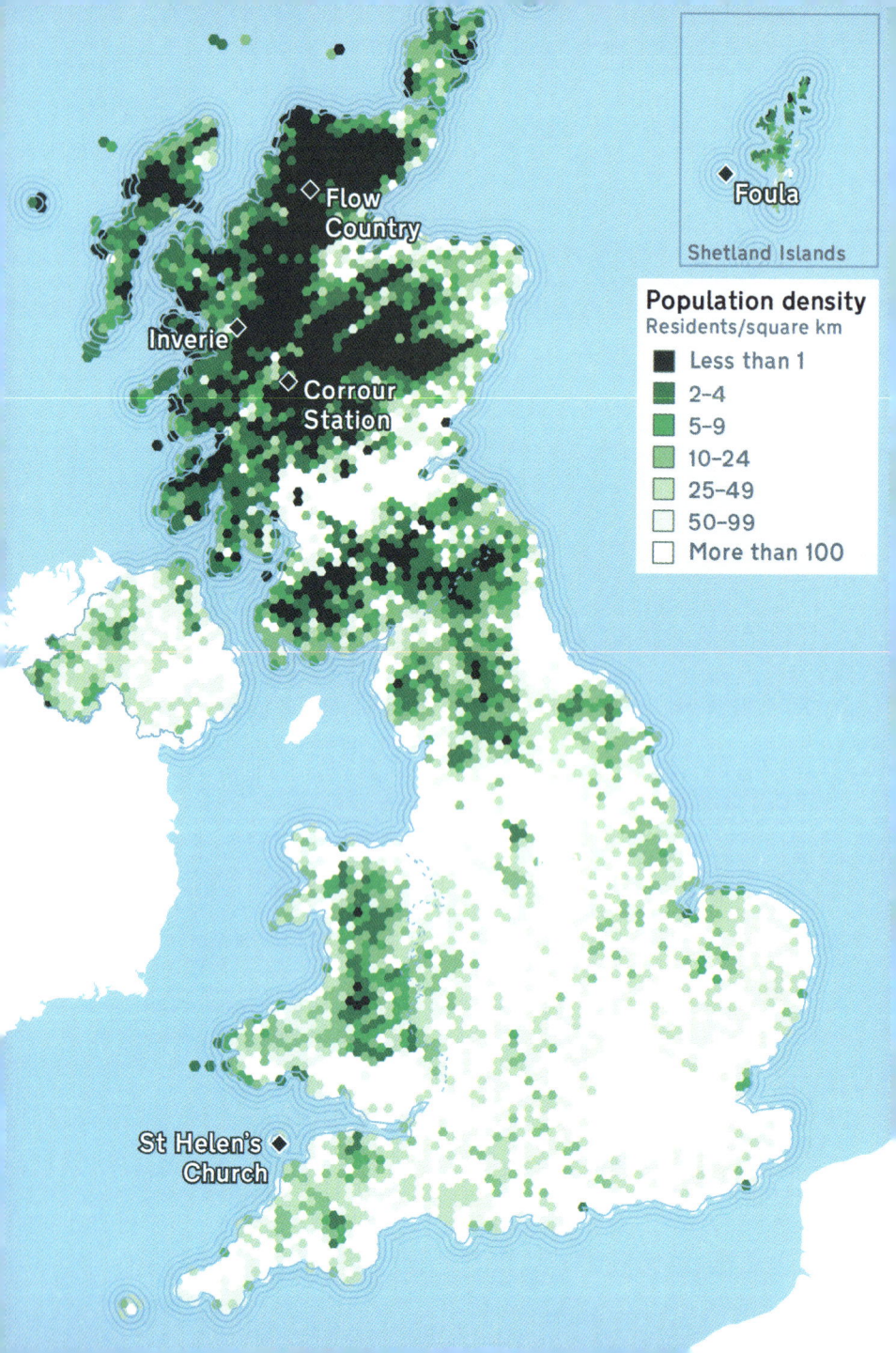

Shetland Islands

Flow Country

Inverie

Corrour Station

Population density
Residents/square km

- Less than 1
- 2–4
- 5–9
- 10–24
- 25–49
- 50–99
- More than 100

St Helen's Church

Fewest people

Around 84 per cent of UK residents live in cities. Because of this, it can be easy to think of the UK as a concrete jungle with people packed in traffic jams or crowded into tube carriages. However, the reality is different: 30 per cent of the UK has a population density of fewer than ten people per km^2 (0.4 sq. mile) – and for 11 per cent the density is lower than one.

In general, the population density of the UK inverts with elevation. Lowland areas – like the south-east of England and Scotland's Central Belt – support a higher population, while upland areas – the Highlands, Mid Wales and the Lake District, to name but a few – are more sparsely populated. This is due to upland areas typically having colder temperatures, thinner air, steeper land for building and less fertile soil – as well as the human aversion to walking up hills.

Foula, in the Shetland Islands, is considered the most remote yet permanently inhabited island of the UK, with just 30 residents. Foula folk still follow the Julian calendar – meaning they celebrate Christmas Day on 6 January! On the Scottish mainland, Inverie is one of the most remote villages – it cannot be reached by car, only by boat or a two-day hike. It is home to the Old Forge, the UK's most remote pub – and you'll be needing a drink after that hike.

The largest uninhabited area is in Caithness and Sutherland. The Flow Country is the largest stretch of blanket bog in Europe. This is a crucial environment for our climate and is estimated to store around 400 million tonnes of carbon.

Other remote locations include St Helen's on Lundy Island – the UK's most remote church – and Corrour Station in the Scottish Highlands, a location so remote that it can't be reached by road.

Darkest spots

Have you ever been walking home late at night, gazed up at the night sky and seen ... nothing? While you may think that this is due to the seemingly constant blanket of grey cloud sitting over the UK, it is more likely due to light pollution.

It's estimated that 85 per cent of the UK has never experienced a sky dark enough to see the Milky Way. While light pollution is more common in large towns and cities, it's not limited to these areas. Towards the north-east of this map, you can see evidence of light pollution across the North Sea, where oil rigs and wind turbines are active around the clock.

Not only is this terrible news for someone trying the age-old trick of impressing their date by pretending to know the constellations of stars, it disrupts the behaviour of wildlife and causes havoc with our circadian rhythm, which is how we know when to go to sleep.

The good news? There are widespread efforts to improve this. Several areas of the UK have been designated as Dark Sky Parks or Reserves. A notable example is Northumberland Dark Sky Park, which is famed for having the darkest skies in Europe. Other similar areas include the Brecon Beacons Dark Sky Reserve, Galloway Forest Dark Sky Park and the Moffat Dark Sky community. Many local councils have committed to improving their light pollution, and the rise of community stargazing events – like Kielder Forest Stargazing and the annual Perseid Meteor Shower viewing in the Brecon Beacons – means that communities and councils alike are starting to foster real change.

So, the next time you're out after dark, try turning off your phone and looking up – who knows what you'll see?

Night time light
Average radiance
nW/cm

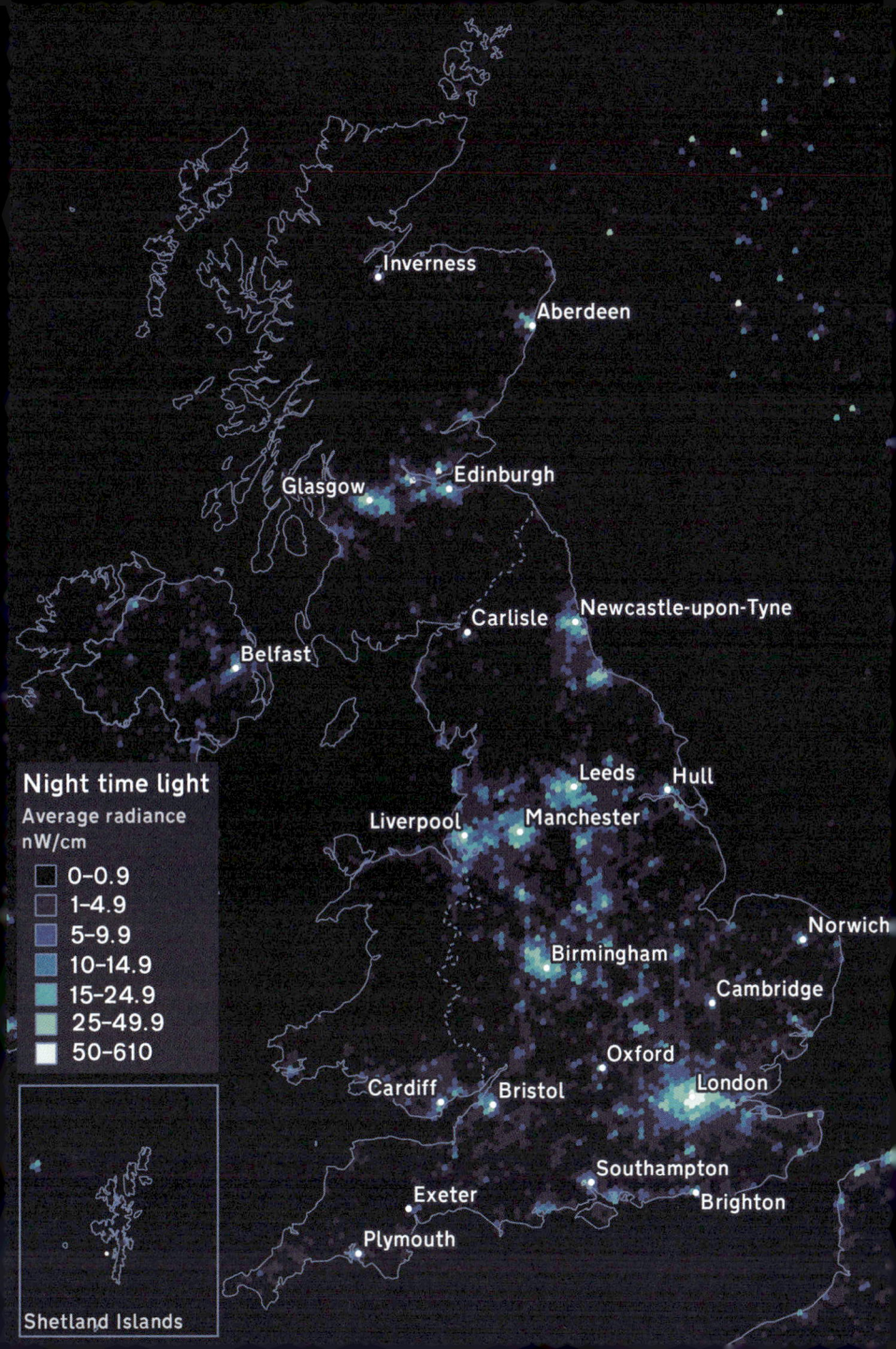

- 0–0.9
- 1–4.9
- 5–9.9
- 10–14.9
- 15–24.9
- 25–49.9
- 50–610

Shetland Islands

Inverness
Aberdeen
Glasgow
Edinburgh
Carlisle
Newcastle-upon-Tyne
Belfast
Leeds
Hull
Liverpool
Manchester
Birmingham
Norwich
Cambridge
Oxford
London
Cardiff
Bristol
Southampton
Brighton
Exeter
Plymouth

Heritage
& History

Shipwrecks, steam trains and some very old pubs – a cartographic journey through the UK's past

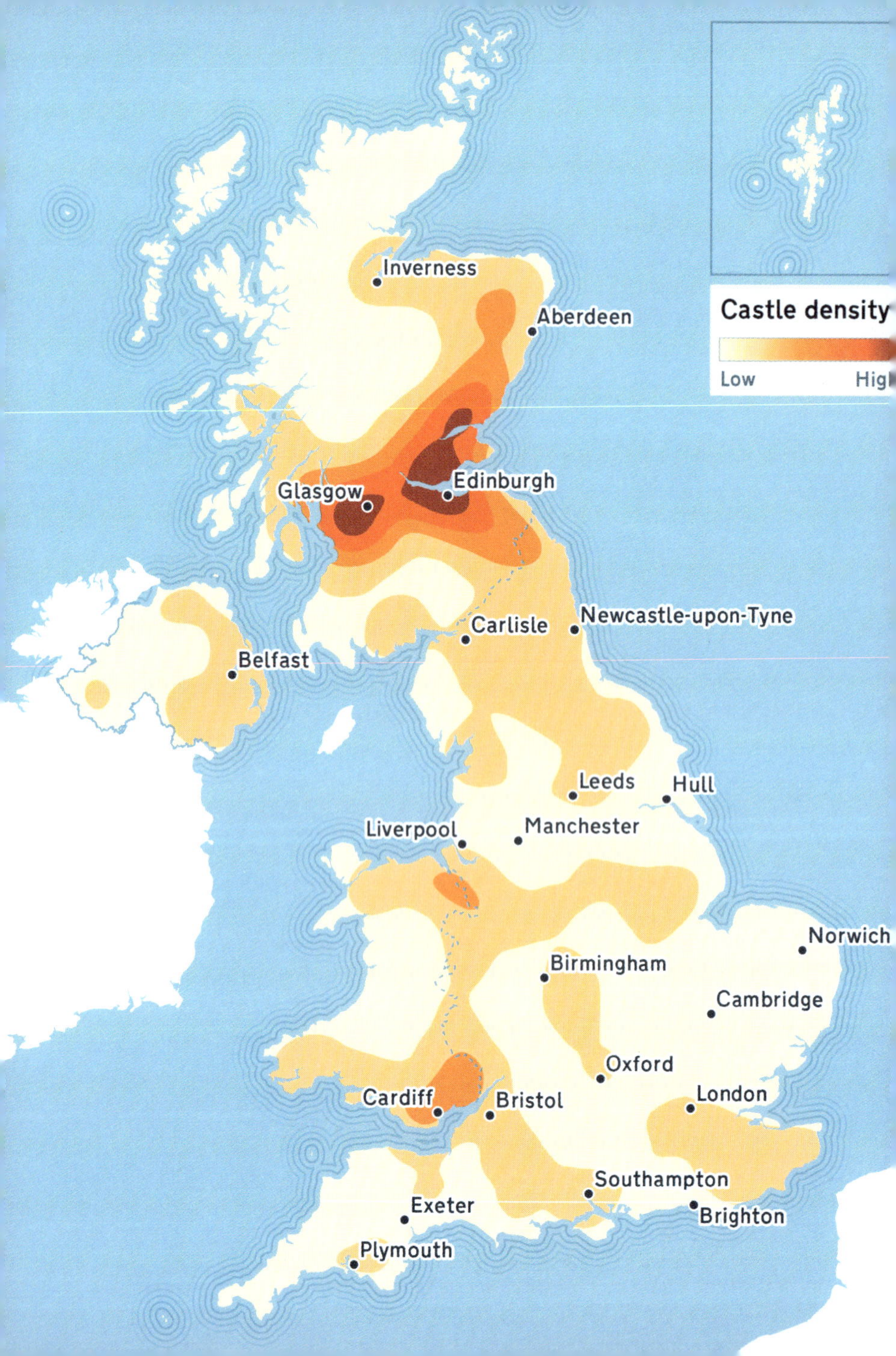
Castle density
Low
Hig
Inverness
Aberdeen
Edinburgh
Glasgow
Carlisle
Newcastle-upon-Tyne
Belfast
Leeds
Hull
Liverpool
Manchester
Norwich
Birmingham
Cambridge
Oxford
Cardiff
Bristol
London
Southampton
Brighton
Exeter
Plymouth

Highest concentration of castles

The UK is thought to be home to as many as 4,000 castles.

These range from magnificent sites like the imposing Bodiam Castle in East Sussex, through to atmospheric and picturesque ruins like Dunseverick Castle in County Antrim, right down to perhaps Britain's smallest castle – the one-bedroom Doyden Castle in Cornwall.

One of Wales's many claims to fame is being the 'Castle capital of the world', boasting over 600 castles (although only around 100 of these are still standing). This is due to Wales's rich history of internal and external power struggles. Following the Norman invasion of 1066, a series of defensive castles – such as Chepstow Castle, built in 1067 – were erected as a means of maintaining control along the Anglo-Welsh border. In the 13th century, the English King Edward I aimed to secure his rule of Wales by building a series of castles known as the Ring of Iron. Many of these can still be visited to this day, including Caernarfon and Conwy castles.

However, beyond Wales this map also shows the great density of castles in Scotland's Central Belt, which runs between Edinburgh and Glasgow. Historically, this region was the political and economic heart of Scotland – making control of it vital in any internal or external power struggle. The building of castles was particularly championed by King David I who ruled in the 12th century, during which time Edinburgh, Stirling and Roxburgh castles were all built.

Notable National Trust places

While we aren't unique in the way we celebrate historic buildings and nature in this country, there is something uniquely British about the way we do it.

For some, a trip to a National Trust property is a bank holiday ritual. From waking up unnecessarily early to beat the traffic, to packing for almost every weather eventuality – raincoat? Check. SPF 50? Check. Woolly hat? You never know! You then spend the next few hours exploring every nook and cranny of your nearest 'I never knew this was here!' National Trust spot, before the inevitable call of a scone and a cup of tea becomes too strong.

The National Trust, which cares for sites across England, Wales and Northern Ireland, was founded in 1895 under the full – albeit slightly less catchy – name of 'The National Trust for Places of Historic Interest and Natural Beauty'. The National Trust for Scotland, which was founded 36 years later, is a different organisation altogether so is not covered here.

As Europe's biggest conservation charity, the National Trust looks after more than 500 historic houses and gardens, nearly 1,000 miles of land and over 700 miles of coastline. As well as the notable locations covered on this map, some of the stranger highlights include a Grade I-listed dog kennel, a rotating shed, a mansion so big that no one's sure how many rooms it has (maybe 400?), an upside-down lighthouse and a beach that squeaks when you walk on it.

Most visitors
Giant's Causeway

Smallest propert
Hawker's Hu

Radio discovered
Poldhu Cove

Map of National Trust Sites

- **First hydroelectric dam** — Cragside
- **Tallest tree Grand Fir** — Skelghyll Woods
- **Largest country house** — Wentworth Woodhouse
- **First land** — Dinas Oleu
- **Most scones served** — Calke Abbey
- **Anglo-Saxon burial site** — Sutton Hoo
- **Largest waterfall** — Henrhyd Falls
- **Most filmed location** — Ashridge Estate
- **First woman MP** — Cliveden
- **First electric Lighthouse** — South Foreland
- **Largest estate** — Holnicote
- **First property** — Alfriston Clergy House
- **Longest beach** — Studland
- **Largest maze** — Glendurgan

Shipwreck sites

Did you know there are 33,019 shipwrecks within 100 miles (160km) of the UK?

Of these, around half (15,923) can be found within just 10 miles (16km) of the shore – something to think about next time you're at the beach enjoying your I-remember-when-it-cost-99p Flake.

So where are these shipwrecks? The short answer: everywhere! Shipwrecks can be found along every stretch of the UK coastline, but there are some particularly treacherous waters. The area stretching from Calais in France, past Broadstairs in Kent and up to Ipswich in Suffolk, has the highest density of shipwrecks – unsurprising, considering the historical importance of the Thames Estuary. Two other port cities with a high number of shipwrecks surrounding them are Southampton and Liverpool.

Danger also lies off the Cornish coast. The seas are so littered with wrecks that the coast is filled with ominously named regions such as 'the Doom Bar' – an area off North Cornwall with large tidal ranges and deceptively shallow waters – and the 'graveyard of ships' off the Lizard Peninsula, a name that speaks for itself. Consider your timbers shivered.

It may not be just danger from the rocks and waves that sailors have had to fear. In the 18th and 19th centuries, fears grew of 'wreckers' – smugglers who deliberately lured ships towards rocky shores in order to profit from the treasure and goods on board.

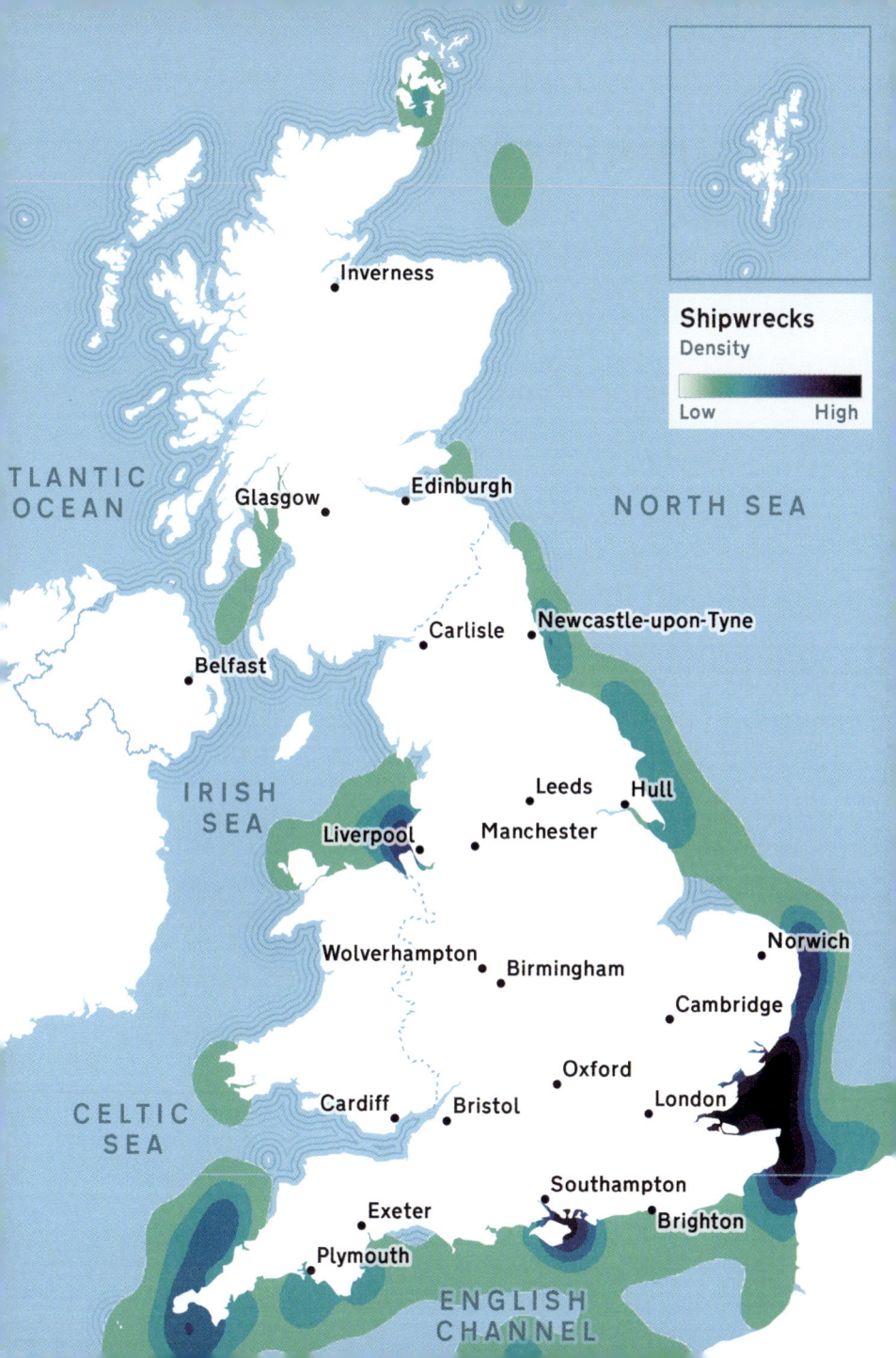

Shipwrecks
Density

Low — High

ATLANTIC OCEAN

NORTH SEA

IRISH SEA

CELTIC SEA

ENGLISH CHANNEL

- Inverness
- Glasgow
- Edinburgh
- Belfast
- Carlisle
- Newcastle-upon-Tyne
- Leeds
- Hull
- Liverpool
- Manchester
- Wolverhampton
- Birmingham
- Norwich
- Cambridge
- Oxford
- London
- Cardiff
- Bristol
- Southampton
- Brighton
- Exeter
- Plymouth

Spookiest spots

A fan of the supernatural? Britain has no end of haunted sites to have you quaking in your boots.

If you're hoping for a ghostly encounter, your best bet may be to head to the oldest pub you can find. One of the most famously haunted sites in Britain is the Skirrid Inn, Abergavenny, Wales – a former courthouse and jail turned pub. Patrons have reported glasses flying across the bar, creepy laughter echoing from upstairs, and sudden drops in temperature. The spooky atmosphere is not helped by the wooden beam in the stairwell from which the condemned were actually hanged – it still bears scorch marks from the ropes that were used.

For a more sober spook, you can't beat a castle. There's the eerily named Chillingham Castle in Northumberland, famed for the torture and demise of prisoners throughout the Medieval period, where visitors often report glimpses of ghostly spirits said to wander the corridors. Then there's Corfe Castle in Dorset, where visitors tell of a headless woman stalking the battlements, supposedly executed for an act of treason during the English Civil War.

Perhaps the most prolific ghost of all is Tudor queen Anne Boleyn. Famously beheaded in 1536 by her husband King Henry VIII on the very reasonable charges of treason, adultery and Henry fancying someone else, her ghost is said to haunt multiple locations. These include the Tower of London, Blickling Hall in Norfolk, Hever Castle in Kent, and Hampton Court in the London Borough of Richmond. Busy lady.

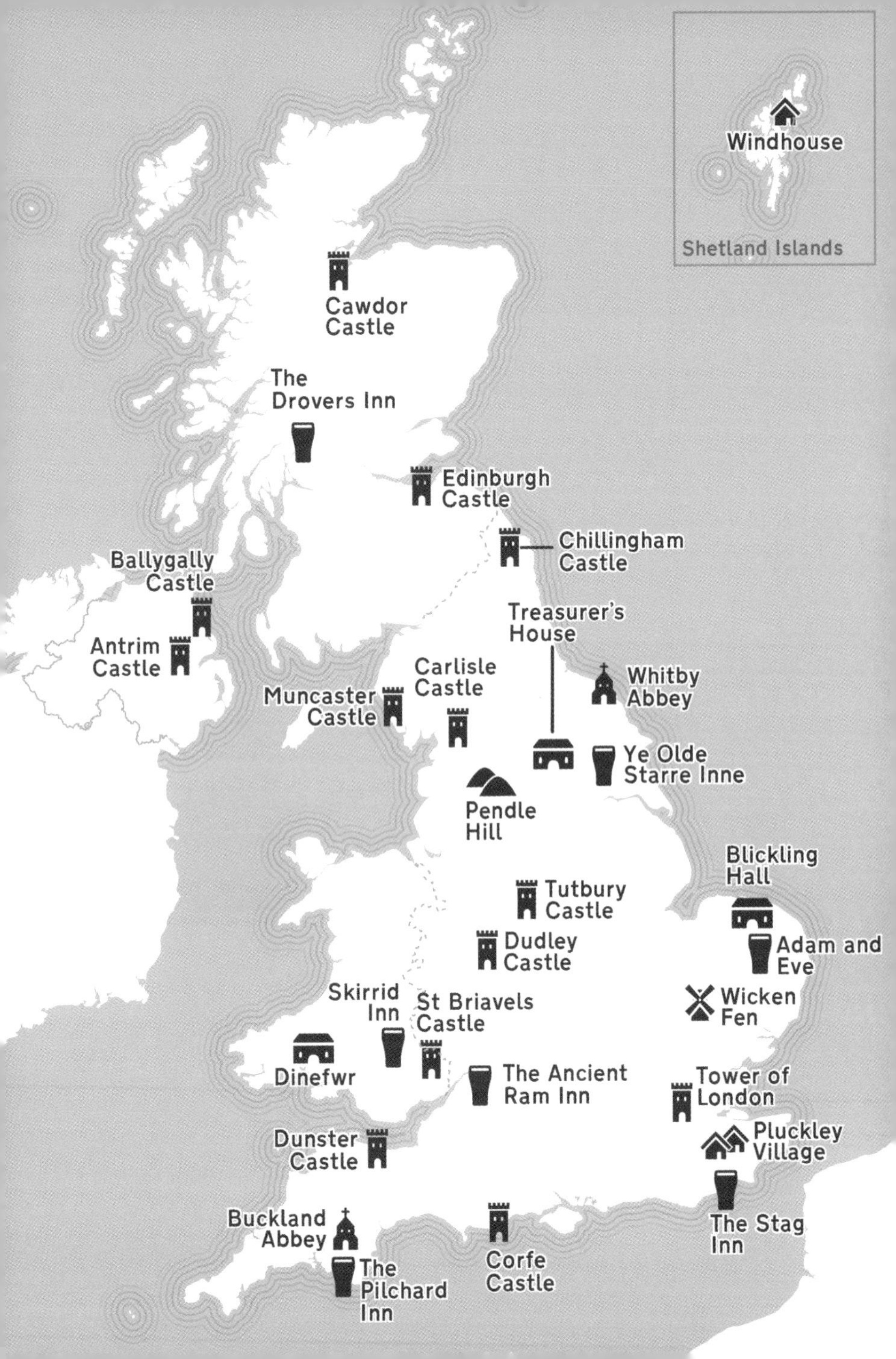

Windhouse

Shetland Islands

Cawdor Castle

The Drovers Inn

Edinburgh Castle

Chillingham Castle

Ballygally Castle

Antrim Castle

Treasurer's House

Muncaster Castle

Carlisle Castle

Whitby Abbey

Ye Olde Starre Inne

Pendle Hill

Blickling Hall

Tutbury Castle

Dudley Castle

Adam and Eve

Skirrid Inn

St Briavels Castle

Wicken Fen

Dinefwr

The Ancient Ram Inn

Tower of London

Pluckley Village

Dunster Castle

Buckland Abbey

The Stag Inn

The Pilchard Inn

Corfe Castle

Heritage rail location
Rail network

Steam trains

Is there anything more romantic than a steam train? It's easy to feel like you're lost in time at the sight of steam billowing around the train's chimney as it starts to build tempo with the warming – forgive the technical term – 'chugga-chugga' sound.

Luckily, even as technology zooms ever onward, the British love of steam trains means that we have maintained many locomotives around the country. In fact, there are over 150 heritage railways across the UK.

The movement to preserve railways started in Wales with the Talyllyn Railway. Originally opened in 1865 to carry slate from the Bryn Eglwys quarries to Tywyn, following years of underinvestment it was preserved through the efforts of volunteers in 1951. Today, it remains a thriving tourist attraction and an inspiration for the preservation of industrial heritage.

Wales is a hub for heritage rail, particularly of the narrow-gauge variety. This term refers to where the track gauge is narrower than the standard 1,435mm (4ft 8½in) gauge. These slimline trains are particularly suited to the tightly winding tracks of the valleys and mountains of Wales.

These stretches of heritage rail are often incredibly scenic, connecting passengers from the mainline network to wilder parts of the UK. For example, the South Devon Railway ferries passengers through picturesque Devon, from Totnes to the foothills of Dartmoor. Further north, the Ravenglass and Eskdale Railway runs from the Cumbrian coast to the valleys of the Lake District, finishing in Dalegarth – just a stone's throw from Scafell Pike (you would have to throw the stone quite high).

Quirkiest museums

When you think about British museums, you probably picture grand Victorian buildings filled with towering dinosaur fossils, ancient pottery and endless paintings of men in rather fetching ruffs. But beyond Britain's famous collections, there is a thriving – and often eccentric – scene of smaller specialist museums.

Many of these celebrate the wonderful every day. From jam to teapots, dog collars to cuckoo clocks – if it exists, there's probably a British museum for it.

At the other end of the scale, there are museums that focus entirely on the fantastical and otherworldly. Take the Museum of Witchcraft and Magic in Cornwall's Boscastle, for example, which houses collections relating to folk magic, Freemasonry and Wicca, and at one time even had a 'resident witch'.

Some museums specialise in bringing together unusual pairings – like the Headhunters Barber Shop and Railway Museum in Enniskillen, County Fermanagh. Who wouldn't want to learn about the arts of hairdressing and locomotion at the same time?

There seems to be a competition for the smallest museum. While you may expect the Smallest House museum in Conwy to take the prize, there is one even tinier: the Warley Museum in West Yorkshire exists within the confines of a red telephone box.

Important note: At the time of writing, Port Talbot's Baked Bean Museum of Excellence – captained by its beloved owner Captain Beany – is relocating, but nonetheless worth mentioning.

- The Scottish Crannog Centre
- Scotland's Secret Bunker
- Rothesay Victorian Toilets
- Headhunters Barber Shop and Railway Museum
- Derwent Pencil Museum
- British Lawnmower Museum
- Warley Museum
- The Smallest House in Great Britain
- Cuckooland
- The Bubblecar Museum
- Pen Museum
- National Gas Museum
- Museum of Carpet
- The National Telephone Kiosk Collection
- Tiptree Jam Museum
- Purton Ships' Graveyard
- The British Dental Museum
- Dog Collar Museum
- Teapot Island
- The Museum of Witchcraft and Magic
- House of Marbles
- The Cartoon Museum
- National Poo Museum

Historic pubs

🍺 30 oldest pubs

- The Sheep Heid Inn, 1360
- Ye Olde Man & Scythe, 1251
- The Bingley Arms, 953
- Scotch Piper Inn, 1320
- Ye Olde Kings Head, 1208
- The White Lion Inn, 722
- A — Ye Olde Trip to Jerusalem, 1189
- B — Ye Olde Salutation Inn, 1240
- C — The Angel and Royal, 1203
- D — The George, 947
- The Old Crown, 1368
- Adam and Eve, 1249
- Skirrid Inn, 1110
- The Porch House, 947
- The Old Ferry Boat Inn, 560
- Ye Olde Fighting Cocks, 793
- The Old House, 1147
- The White Hart, 1216
- Blue Anchor Inn, 1380
- E — The Old Bell, 1120
- F — The Bear Inn, 1242
- G — Turf Tavern, 1381
- H — The Royal Standard of England, 1086
- Three Crowns, 1200s
- The George Inn, 1397
- The Red Lion, 1148
- The Crown Inn, 1383
- The Lamb, 1180
- The Mermaid Inn, 1156

Oldest pubs

If there's one thing the UK does well, it's proper old pubs. The crackling fire, the old-fashioned beer glasses over the bar, the smell of centuries of spilled ale wafting through the beams ... perfection.

But which pub lays claim to being Britain's oldest? The answer is – of course – contested. Many historic pubs have been burnt down, rebuilt and repurposed. Some stake their claim by when they were first licensed, others by the more dubious record 'that people have been drinking ale in (probably) this location since 1749'.

Officially – officially here meaning 'it's in the *Guinness World Records*' – the honour goes to the Porch House, in the charming Cotswolds market town of Stow-on-the-Wold, which is said to date back to AD 947. This title is contested, however, by many proud historic boozers. One notable claimant is the picture-perfect Old Ferry Boat in St Ives, Cambridgeshire, which claims to date back to AD 560. This means that locals were enjoying a beer here before England even existed!

Many of these pubs aren't simply historic in that they're just really, really old – but that historic things happened in them. Take The George Inn in Norton St Philip, Somerset. Licensed in 1397, around 300 years later it was pivotal in the Monmouth Rebellion against James II – first as a headquarters, then a courtroom and, eventually, as an execution site.

The great thing is, these pubs aren't even rarities. There are around 45,000 pubs across the UK – many of which are centuries old. This map shows just a fraction of these: the 30 oldest pubs in the country – also known as the most historic pub crawl ever.

Food & Drink

Roast dinners, fish and chips and top British bakes – the geography of British taste

Bread roll or bun?

There are few things more likely to get Brits into a passionate debate than the name for the humble bread roll. Bun, bap, batch, cob, barmcake, stotty … There are seemingly endless names for what is essentially flour, yeast and water.

'Roll' seems to be the most pervasive name, but there are pockets of regional variation – such as 'bun' in the north of England and 'cob' in the Midlands. However, these are not as clear-cut as you might expect, and the survey conducted for this book showed a lot of variation, even within relatively small areas.

So, what is causing these differences? There are a few theories. One is the historical origin of each of the terms. For instance, 'batch' is thought to derive from the Anglo-Saxon Germanic *bachen*. Meanwhile, 'roll' is thought to be a product of the French influence of the Norman invaders in the later 11th century.

Another theory is that rolls are named after shapes they resemble. The term preferred in the Midlands – 'cob' – is thought to be due to the resemblance to a cobblestone or a 'cop' (a now-archaic term for 'head').

Historically, Brits were far less likely to move around the country than they are today – and so, over time, distinct regional terms developed.

But could that be changing? Brits are now more inclined than ever to relocate to different places in the UK, particularly towards urban areas. The mass production and packaging of food means that the easiest thing is for a supermarket to call everything a 'roll' and be done with it.

What do you call a bread roll?

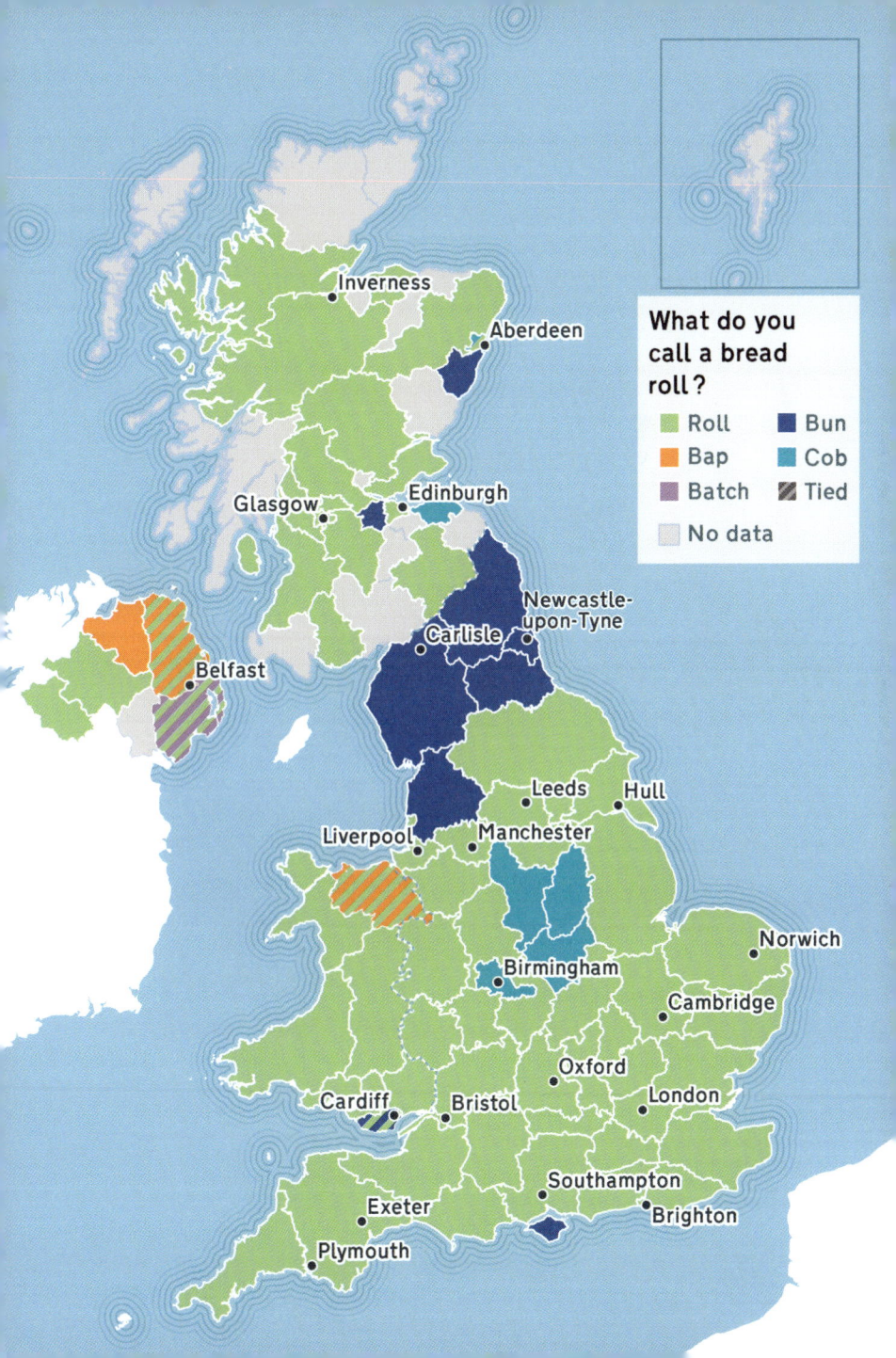

- Roll
- Bap
- Batch
- Bun
- Cob
- Tied
- No data

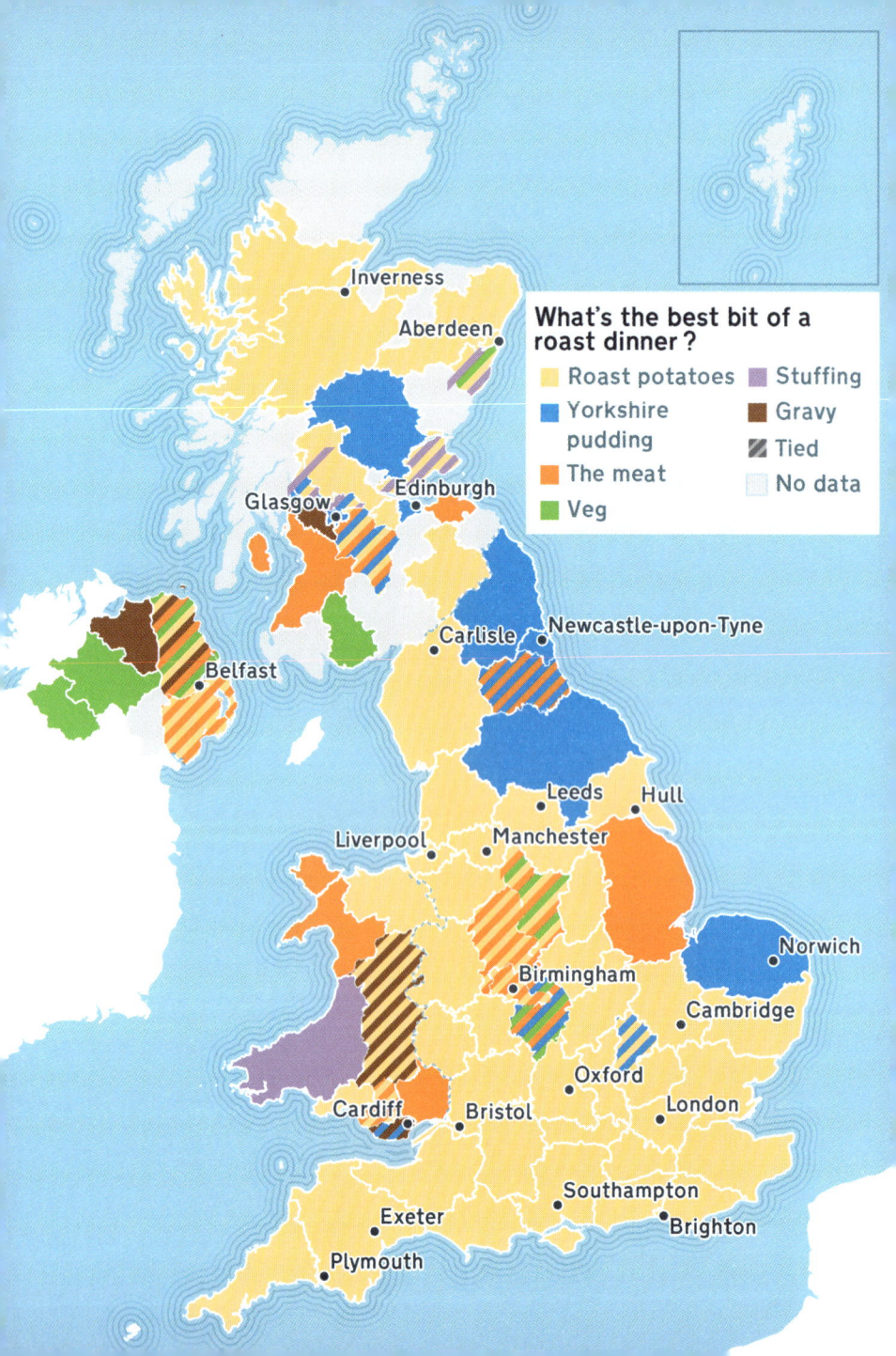

What's the best bit of a roast dinner?

- Roast potatoes
- Yorkshire pudding
- The meat
- Veg
- Stuffing
- Gravy
- Tied
- No data

The best bit of a roast dinner

Outside the UK, British food generally has a bad reputation. Clearly anyone holding this view has never experienced the delights of a roast dinner.

Whether it's enjoyed at the pub after a long walk or while relaxing at home before indulging in an hour-long nap, a roast dinner can't be beaten. Some theories see their origin dating back to medieval times, when serfs would spend their single day off a week practising battle techniques (doesn't sound like much of a day off), and be rewarded with a spit of oxen. Roasts are also believed to have been popularised in the 15th century thanks to the influence of King Henry VII – and yet, somehow, he is less famous than his son.

Roasts became increasingly popular due to the Christian Church banning meat consumption on Friday and imposing a fast before the service on Sunday. By the 1700s, many families would place a cut of meat in the oven before church, which could easily be transformed into a roast dinner feast.

So which is the best part? A comfortable win goes to the roast potato, with differences of opinion across the country. For example, Yorkshire puddings (which seem to baffle non-Brits) are more popular in the north-east.

Note: In this survey, only 'standard' trimmings were included. No Christmas specials such as pigs in blankets or bread sauce were options, and vegetables were grouped together to avoid questions like, 'Are the parsnips honey-roasted? Because that changes things.'

Favourite crisp flavours

Did you know that, in the UK, we eat roughly 6 billion bags of crisps every year? Whether it's grabbing a bag on the go, constructing a crunchy crisp sandwich, or doing the classic rip-down-the-side and share at the pub – nothing hits the spot like a nice bag of crisps. They've been a part of British cuisine since the 1920s, when crisp pioneer Frank Smith produced paper bags filled with crisps, and a sachet of salt to season them yourself.

The humble British crisp has undergone something of a renaissance in recent years. It's now possible to purchase crisps in seemingly every flavour under the sun – from plain to quadruple-cooked. Anyone for a packet of Firecracker Lobster, Oyster and Vinegar or Haggis & Cracked Black Pepper? Then there are the British classics, such as the nuclear Monster Munch, neon Wotsits and somehow-vegetarian Bacon Frazzles.

However, at the heart of the British crisp flavour palette, there are three broad flavours. These are the crowd-pleasing ready-salted (just 'normal' crisps, thank you very much), zingy salt and vinegar, and don't-eat-them-on-public-transport cheese and onion.

But which comes out on top? Salt and vinegar, hands down. Maybe it's the concept of our beloved fish and chips concentrated into one bite-size crunchy snack.

Of the big three, which is your favourite crisp?

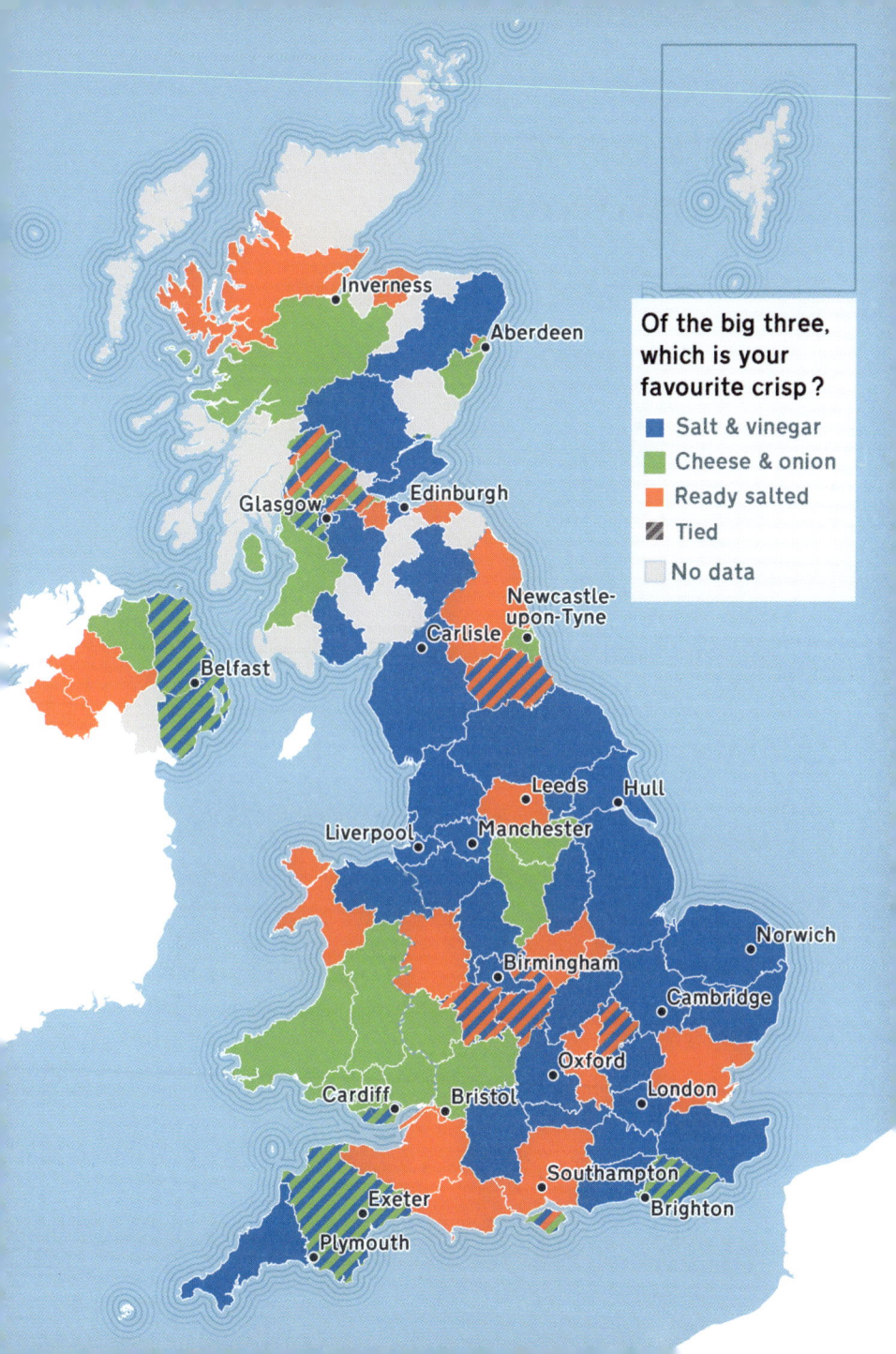

- Salt & vinegar
- Cheese & onion
- Ready salted
- Tied
- No data

Fish and chip shop density

Picture this. It's June. It's Friday evening. The last drops of sunlight are wafting through the kitchen window as you open the fridge to try to invent something for dinner, before shouting, 'Shall we just go to the chippie?'

Fish and chips are an intrinsic part of British life. The fluffy chips, the crisp batter and the industrial-strength smell of vinegar, all make for a perfect, indulgent, entirely beige dinner.

There are over 5,000 dedicated chippies across the country – that's around one shop per 13,000 people. This is – however – far lower than it used to be. Fish and chip shops were at their most popular in the 1920s, when there were estimated to be around 35,000! Fish and chips were one of the few foods to escape rationing during both world wars due to their importance for maintaining morale.

While chippies can be found the length and breadth of the UK, there is something special about enjoying your fish and chips (or battered sausages, of course) by the seaside. This is reflected in the density of chippies in these areas. It's highest in locations just north of Land's End, Cornwall, where the villages of Sennen Cove and Mayon (with a total population of around 350) boast a fish and chip shop each! Conversely, the number of fish and chips shops compared to the population in larger urban areas – such as Greater London and Manchester – is lower, perhaps due to competition from a broader range of fast-food offerings.

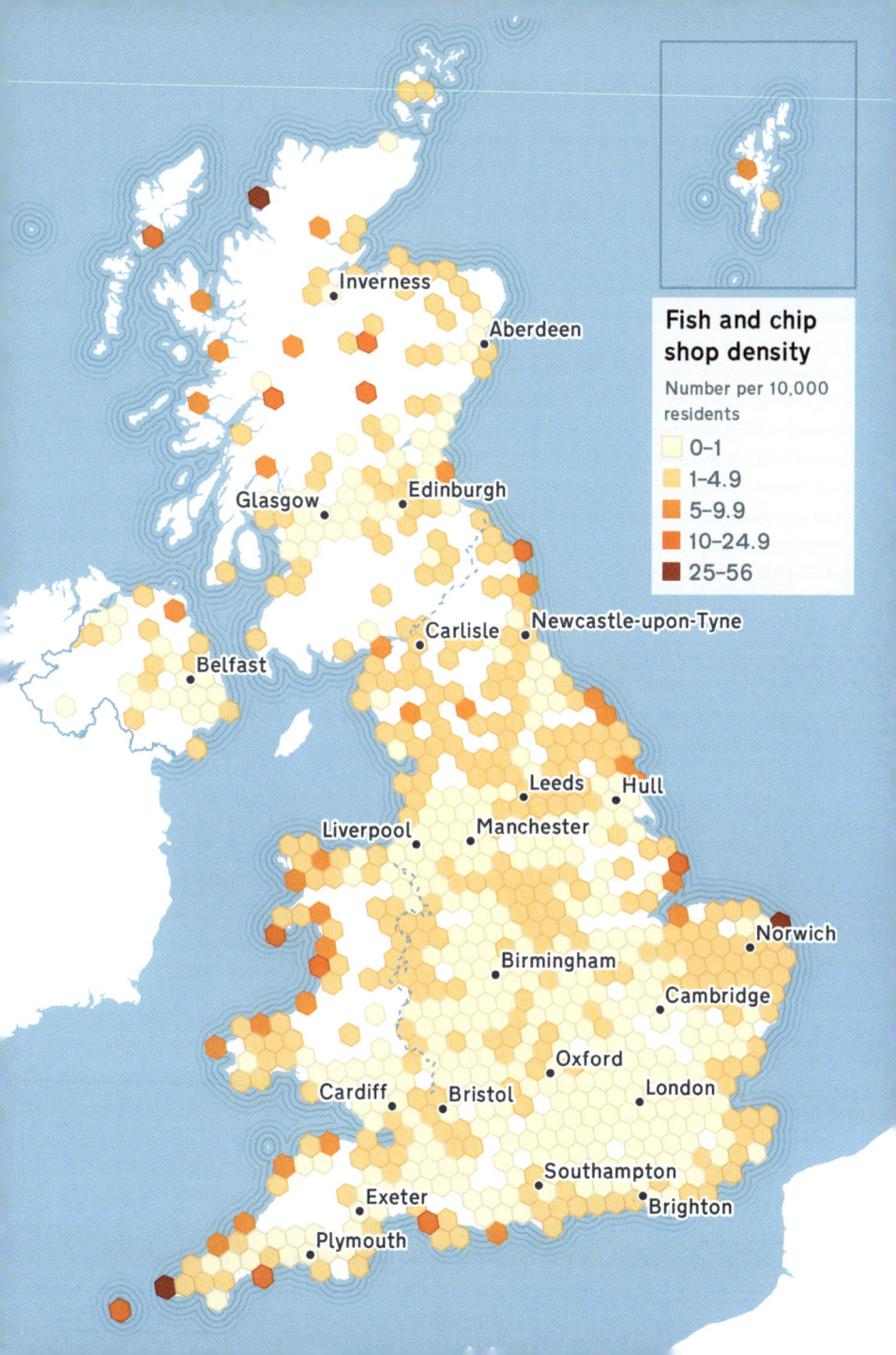

Fish and chip shop density

Number per 10,000 residents

- 0–1
- 1–4.9
- 5–9.9
- 10–24.9
- 25–56

Top chip toppings

The traditional topping for the classic British dish of fish and chips is salt and vinegar, giving the heavy dish its signature tangy kick. This is popular UK-wide, with almost everyone enjoying this option.

Beyond salt and vinegar, other toppings for chips are far more of an acquired taste. For example, ketchup has widespread, yet low-level, support across the whole of the country. In Scotland, niche toppings seem to be the order of the day, with curry sauce, gravy, mushy peas and cheese all having fans.

Beyond these traditional toppings, there are some more unusual ways Brits take their chips. For example, in areas like Yorkshire you can request that your chips be served with 'scraps', 'bits' or 'scrumps' – essentially crispy pieces of batter. And who could say no to a pickled gherkin, onion or egg on the side? Well, quite a lot of people – but the option is always there, sitting behind the till in a jar that wouldn't look out of place in the Natural History Museum.

Curry sauce

Gravy

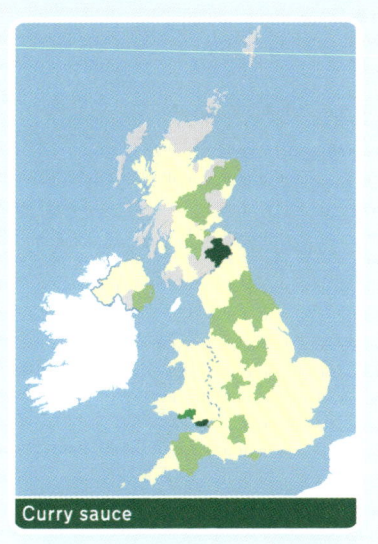

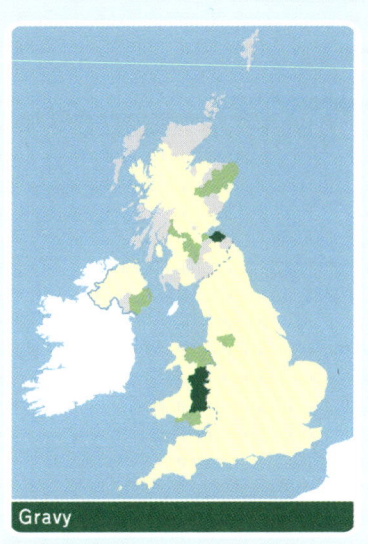

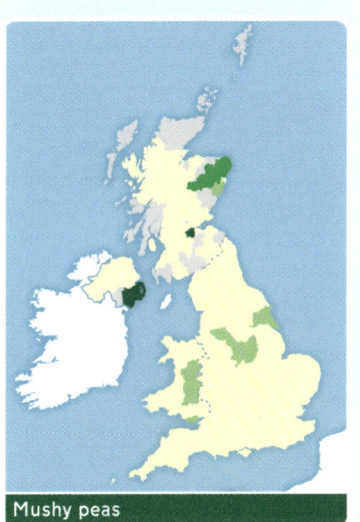

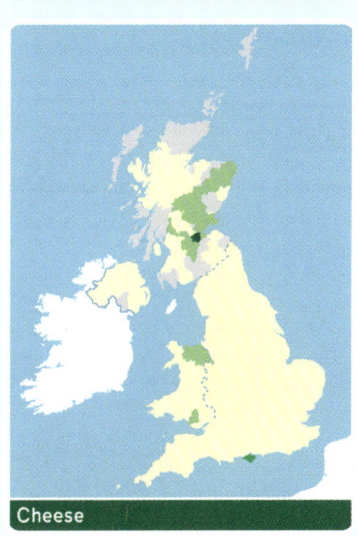

Mushy peas

Cheese

% of people
- 0–24%
- 25–49%
- 50–74%
- 75–100%
- No data

Cornish pasty hotspots

It's unclear when Cornish pasties first came into existence. A letter has been found from the 1530s, which was sent, with a pasty, by King Henry VIII to his then-wife Jane Seymour. Further back, in 1208, pasties are referred to in a charter granted by King John to the town of Great Yarmouth. They became particularly popular in Cornwall during the 17th and 18th centuries; their unique shape meant they could easily be put into a pocket and consumed in the mines.

Throughout their long and storied history, pasties have been fiercely Cornish. In 2011, the European Commission granted Cornish pasties Protected Geographical Indication, joining the ranks of Parmigiano-Reggiano, Scotch whisky and champagne.

This means that a 'proper' pasty must meet certain specifications, including ingredients (25 per cent beef and no artificial flavourings), shape (the distinctive 'D' shape and crucial side crimping – none of

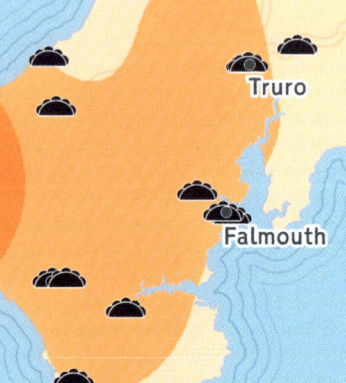

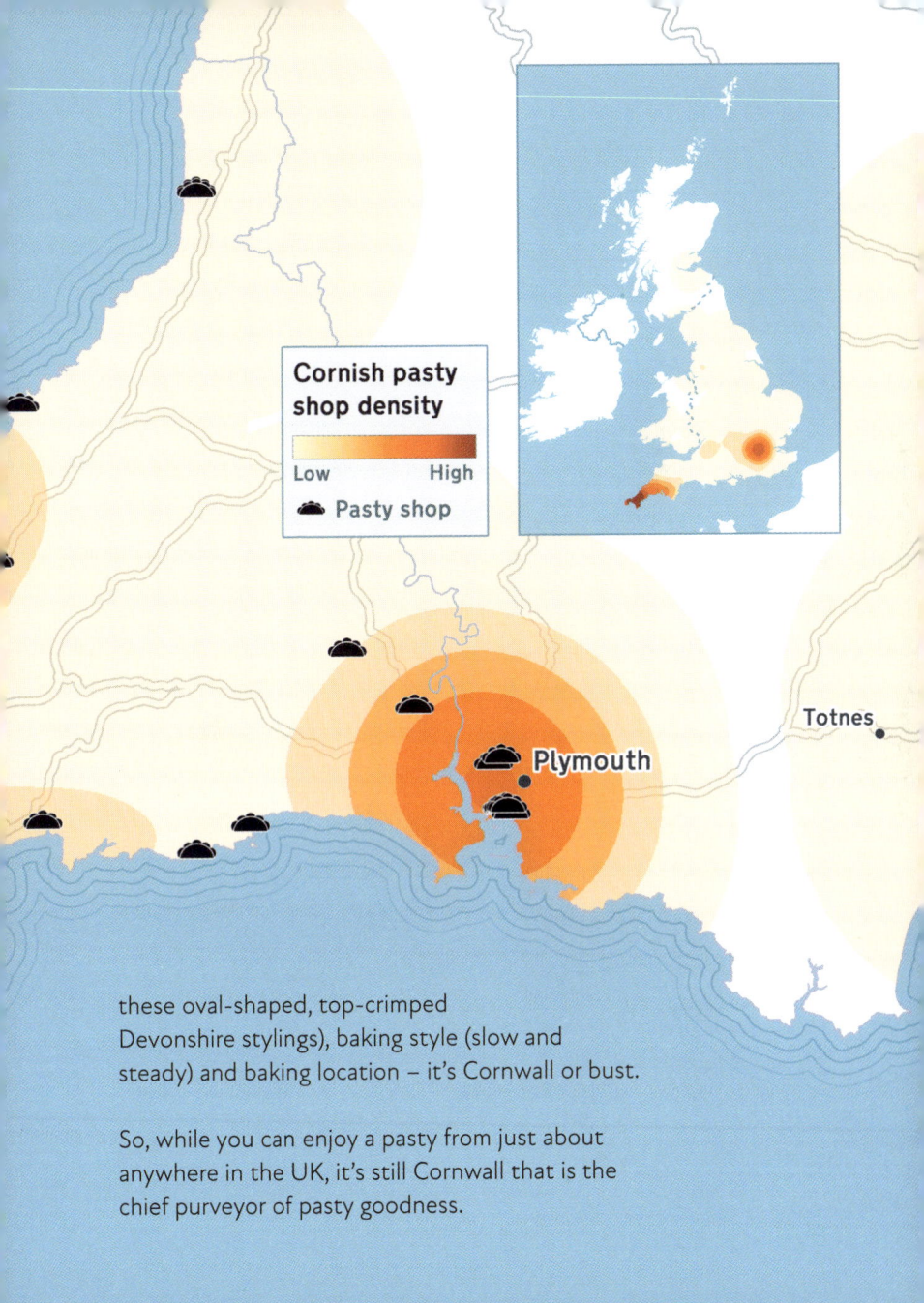

Cornish pasty shop density

Low — High

🥟 Pasty shop

Totnes

Plymouth

these oval-shaped, top-crimped Devonshire stylings), baking style (slow and steady) and baking location – it's Cornwall or bust.

So, while you can enjoy a pasty from just about anywhere in the UK, it's still Cornwall that is the chief purveyor of pasty goodness.

Local bakes

From the Cornish Fairing to Shetland's Reestit Mutton Pie, from Chelsea Buns to Belfast's Fifteens, the UK boasts a great variety of regional baked goods. These biscuits, pastries and pies have become a symbol of local identity, with residents taking fierce pride in them.

This variety stems from many towns historically having a bakers guild, each favouring distinctive local cuisines. As the UK industrialised in the 18th century, portable baked goods grew in popularity as they were the easiest way to fill up throughout the day. Even today, when many Brits have traded the factory for the office, you still can't beat the convenience of a scotch egg or a pork pie.

Many local bakes were developed as a means of taking advantage of local ingredients. For example, Scotland is prime oat-growing territory enabling flour-rich bakes, such as the Abernethy Biscuit. Meanwhile, in Northern Ireland, potatoes are a popular ingredient leading to the famous Irish Tattie Bread.

This rich history has led to a great diversity in British bakes. In the present day, the tradition of baking is still alive and well – especially following the Covid-19 lockdowns of 2020–21. According to Britain Loves Baking, a massive 71 per cent of Brits are reported to be baking weekly (up from 31 per cent pre-pandemic), with baking (and, of course, eating!) providing comfort and helping people to feel more connected to each other.

Local bakes of the United Kingdom

Legend — Local bakes:
- Biscuits
- Breads & buns
- Cakes
- Desserts
- Pastries
- Tarts
- Pies & pasties
- Sweets

- Reestit Mutton Pie — Shetland Islands
- Forfar Bridie — Forfar
- Dundee Cake — Dundee
- Abernethy Biscuits — Abernethy
- Ecclefechan Tart — Ecclefechan
- Bannock — Selkirk
- Yellowman — Ballycastle
- Fifteens — Belfast
- Tattie Bread — County Down
- Sticky Toffee Pudding — Lake District
- Fat Rascal — Whitby
- Goosnargh Cake — Goosnargh
- Kendal Mint Cake — Kendal
- Yorkshire Curd Tart — Yorkshire
- Eccles Cake — Salford
- Chorley Cake — Chorley
- Anglesey Cake — Llangefni
- Manchester Tart — Manchester
- Liverpool Tart — Merseyside
- Bakewell Tart — Bakewell
- Cambridge Burnt Cream — Cambridge
- Aberffraw Biscuit — Aberffraw
- Llangollen Pudding — Llangollen
- Teisen Lap — Blaenau Ffestiniog
- Coventry Godcakes — Coventry
- Norfolk Treacle Tart — Norfolk
- Shrewsbury Cake — Shrewsbury
- Banbury Cake — Banbury
- Bedfordshire Clanger — Bedfordshire
- Suffolk Rusk — Suffolk
- Monmouth Pudding — Monmouth
- Tottenham Cake — Tottenham
- Glamorgan Tart — Glamorgan
- Bath Bun — Bath
- Chelsea Bun — London
- Lardy Cake — Wiltshire
- Gypsy Tart — Isle of Sheppey
- Banoffee Pie — Jevington
- Cornish Pasty — Cornwall
- Cornish / Devonshire Split — Cornwall / Devon
- Dorset Apple Cake — Dorset
- Cornish Fairing — Truro

Scone pronunciation

It's time for the big one. Arguments about football or politics pale in comparison to the most divisive debate in the UK: how do you pronounce 'scone'?

For some, it's pronounced like 'gone'. For others, it's more like 'cone'. The 'gone' pronunciation is more common across Northern Ireland, Scotland, Wales and Northern England. 'Cone' pronouncers can be more commonly found in the south and the Midlands. However, this is not a clear-cut regional divide, and in fact the different versions appear across all corners of the UK.

Many believe the pronunciation has more to do with social class than geography, with the 'cone' version being deemed the 'posher' scone. However, the Royal family are said to prefer the 'gone' version – and does it really get posher than that?

There's also the village of Scone and nearby Scone Palace (where early Kings of Scotland were crowned), which is pronounced 'skoon' … but let's not go there.

No matter how it's pronounced, Brits can all agree on one thing: it would be absolute madness to call scones biscuits and eat them with gravy, like they do across the pond.

How do you say 'scone?'

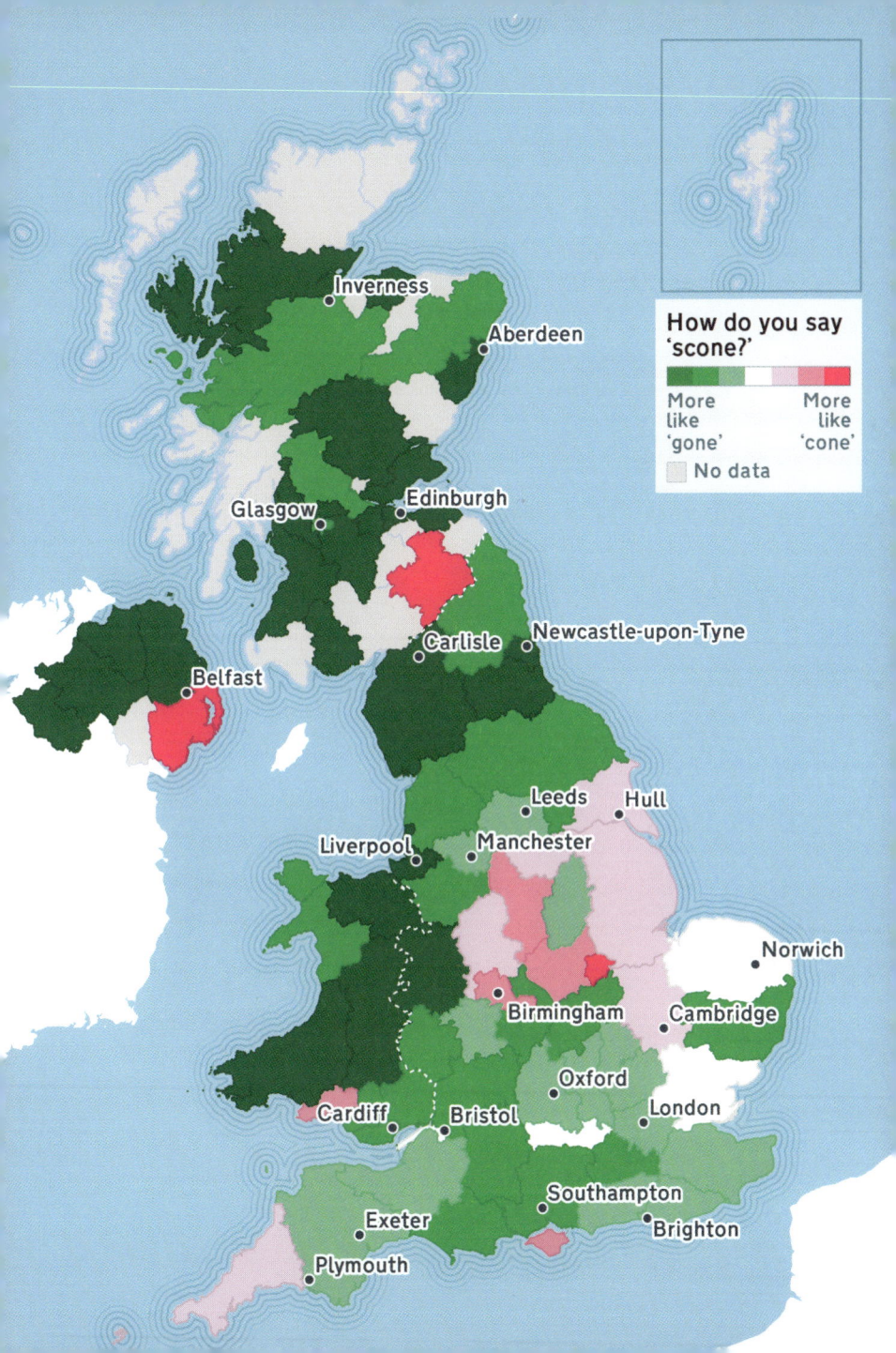

More like 'gone' — More like 'cone'

No data

The cream tea: what goes first?

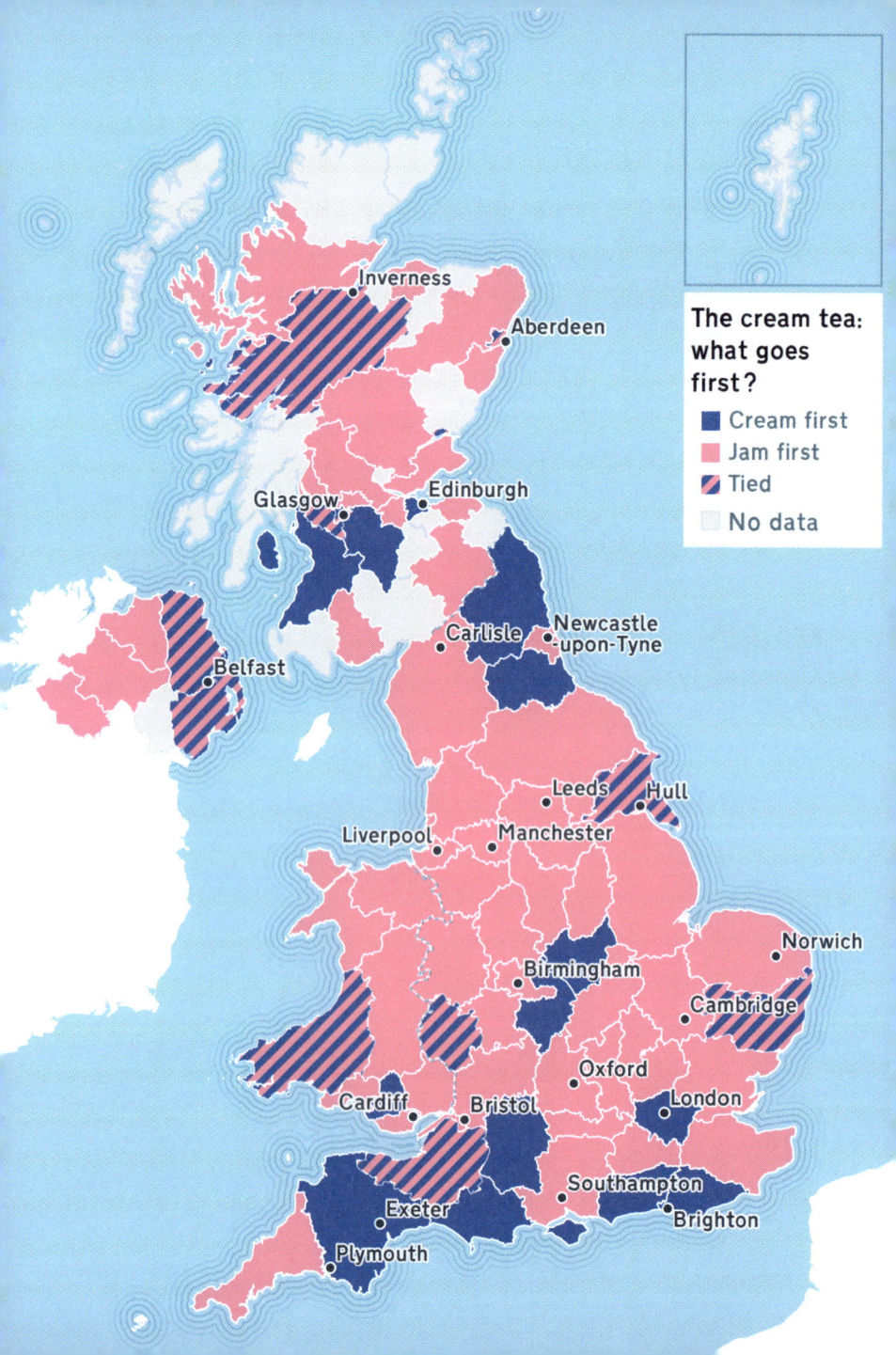

- Cream first
- Jam first
- Tied
- No data

Jam before cream, or cream before jam?

Nothing says 'summer holidays' quite like a cream tea. That feeling of slicing open a freshly-baked scone and picking up your knife to spread ... what? Cream first, or jam first? That's the debate that has originated from the depths of the West Country. The 'Cornish way' stipulates that jam should go first, the idea behind this being that it allows the sweetness of jam to shine through the richness of the clotted cream. Over the Tamar, Devonians prefer the 'cream first' method, more akin to buttering toast, before adding the jam.

This debate goes all the way to the top. In 1993, it was reported that Queen Elizabeth II was decidedly in the jam-first camp.

The majority of the UK seems to side with the Cornish – jam belongs first. However, pockets of disagreement exist and it's clear we all need to hunker down and do far more research on the topic.

Plants & Animals

From ancient trees to tiny robins –
our most beloved flora and fauna

Tree type
- 🌳 Oak
- 🌳 Yew

Fortingall Yew — 2,000–9,000 years

Belvoir Oak — 500–700 years

Borrowdale Yews — >1,500 years

Crom Yews — >800 years

Major Oak — 800–1,100 years

Llangernyw Yew — 4,000–5,000 years

Marton Oak — 1,200 years

Bowthorpe Oak — >1,000 years

Quarry Oak — 1,000 years

Defynnog Yew — 2,000–3,000 years

Ankerwycke Yew — 2,500 years

Big Belly Oak — 1,000–1,100 years

Crowhurst Yew — 4,000 years

King Offa's Oak — 1,300–1,500 years

Oldest trees

Around 9,000 years ago, the UK looked completely different. Britain was still physically connected to mainland Europe through a low-lying stretch of land called Doggerland, and residents spent most of their time hunting, gathering and waiting for television to be invented.

It was about this time that the UK's oldest living 'thing' came into existence: the Fortingall Yew. This tree can be found in a churchyard in Perthshire, with estimates dating it to between 2,000 and 9,000 years old.

While the Fortingall Yew takes the crown for the UK's oldest tree, ancient trees can be found in all corners of the country. In fact, ancient woodlands – defined as areas that have been continuously wooded since 1600 (or 1750 in Scotland) – cover around 2.5 per cent of the UK. They are crucial to the health of our ecosystem and are considered one of the most biodiverse land-based habitats, supporting a huge range of rare flora and fauna.

Yews and oaks are best equipped for thriving for hundreds – or even thousands – of years. Yews in particular are adept at this, having developed a system whereby older parts of the tree die, to be replaced by younger shoots that regenerate at the bottom of the tree, which sounds an awful lot like cheating.

UK dog breed map

From the stout Bulldog to the petite Yorkshire Terrier, around 80 dog breeds are thought to originate from the UK. While in some cases the exact origin of many British breeds is lost in the mists of time, there are some breeds whose origin can be pinpointed to specific counties, towns or even houses. These can be explored on the next page, and include Golden Retrievers (Guisachan House, Inverness-shire), Gordon Setters (Gordon Castle, Moray) and Clumber Spaniels (Clumber Park, Nottinghamshire).

Why does such a small island boast such dog diversity? As a nation of dog lovers, we have a long history of selective breeding to ensure dogs are the best suited to meet local needs. Pembroke and Cardigan Welsh Corgis became invaluable to farmers in West Wales who found this hardy breed well suited to herding cattle while being small enough to duck under any errant kicks. Meanwhile, Cairn Terriers are enthusiastic diggers, giving them an innate talent for digging out small, furry prey in the rocky Scottish landscape.

This enthusiasm for selective breeding was particularly fervent in the late 19th century, with a growing interest in the practice being linked to Victorian ideas of class. It was during this time that The Kennel Club – the oldest kennel club in the world – was founded and held its first show at Crystal Palace in London in 1873.

These days, dogs are less likely to be bred for their ability to sniff out game, and more for their appearance and personality. With around 38,000 registrations, the Labrador Retriever is the UK's most popular dog, beloved for its trainability, intelligence and gentle nature. Other popular breeds include the Instagrammable French Bulldog, inexhaustible Cocker Spaniel and small-yet-sturdy Miniature Smooth Haired Dachshund.

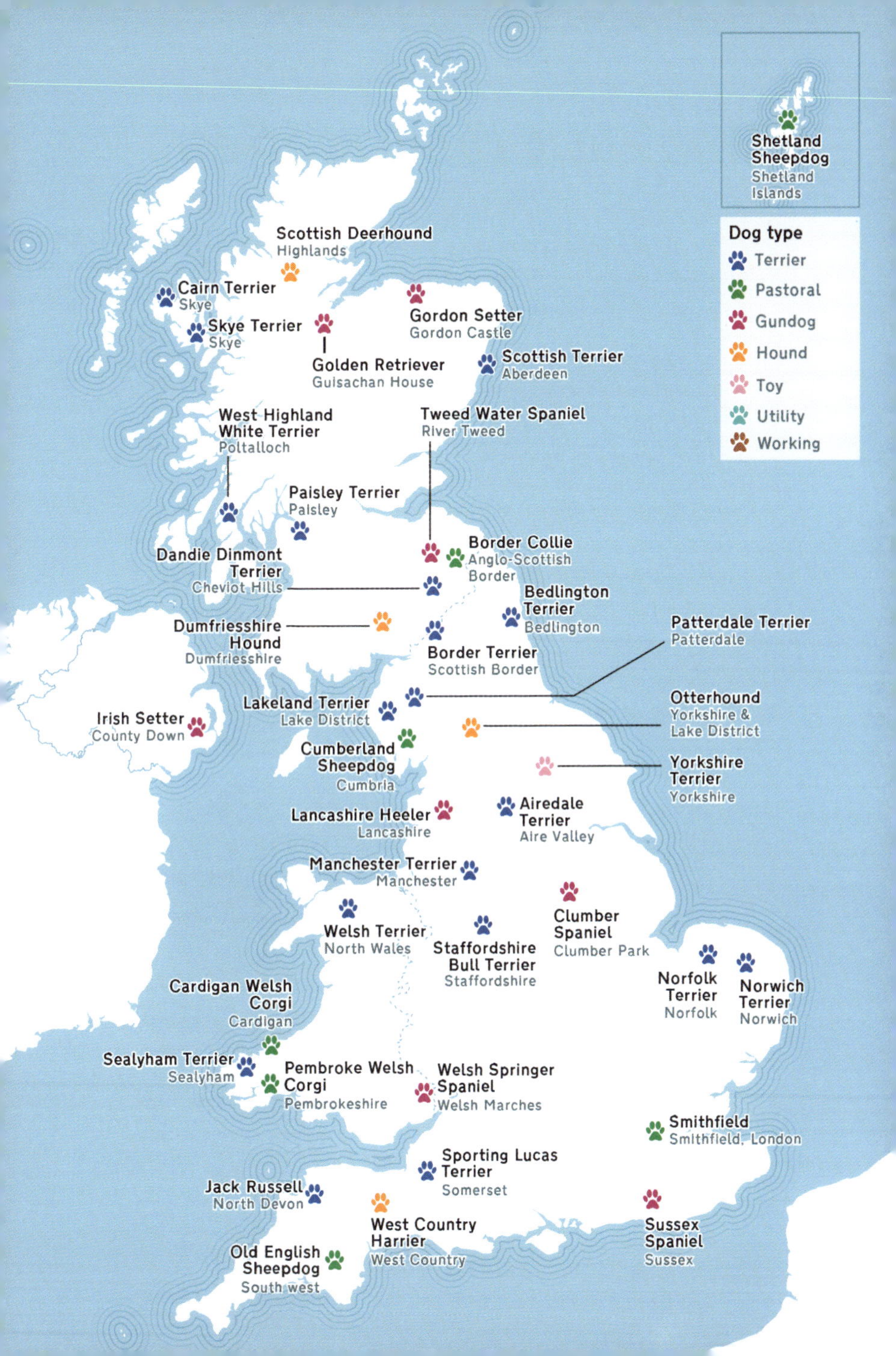
Shetland Sheepdog
Shetland Islands
Dog type
Terrier
Pastoral
Gundog
Hound
Toy
Utility
Working
Scottish Deerhound
Highlands
Cairn Terrier
Skye
Skye Terrier
Skye
Gordon Setter
Gordon Castle
Golden Retriever
Guisachan House
Scottish Terrier
Aberdeen
West Highland White Terrier
Poltalloch
Tweed Water Spaniel
River Tweed
Paisley Terrier
Paisley
Border Collie
Anglo-Scottish Border
Dandie Dinmont Terrier
Cheviot Hills
Bedlington Terrier
Bedlington
Dumfriesshire Hound
Dumfriesshire
Border Terrier
Scottish Border
Patterdale Terrier
Patterdale
Otterhound
Yorkshire & Lake District
Lakeland Terrier
Lake District
Irish Setter
County Down
Cumberland Sheepdog
Cumbria
Yorkshire Terrier
Yorkshire
Lancashire Heeler
Lancashire
Airedale Terrier
Aire Valley
Manchester Terrier
Manchester
Clumber Spaniel
Clumber Park
Welsh Terrier
North Wales
Staffordshire Bull Terrier
Staffordshire
Norfolk Terrier
Norfolk
Norwich Terrier
Norwich
Cardigan Welsh Corgi
Cardigan
Sealyham Terrier
Sealyham
Pembroke Welsh Corgi
Pembrokeshire
Welsh Springer Spaniel
Welsh Marches
Smithfield
Smithfield, London
Sporting Lucas Terrier
Somerset
Jack Russell
North Devon
West Country Harrier
West Country
Sussex Spaniel
Sussex
Old English Sheepdog
South west

Dinosaur discoveries

Did you know there have been around 430 dinosaur fossil discoveries in the UK? The vast majority of these are in England, with 71 (16.3 per cent) found on the famous Jurassic Coast, between Dorset's Lyme Regis and Swanage. Of these, 27 are from the Jurassic period proper, with 38 coming from the later Cretaceous period. However, the 'Cretaceous Coast' may be slightly less marketable without its own cinematic universe.

Other hotspots are Yorkshire's Dinosaur Coast, stretching between Whitby and Flamborough Head, and the Isles of Wight and Skye.

On this map you can see where fossils can be found depending on their time period. Fossils from the earlier Triassic period (245–208 million years ago), are more typical in the West Country, particularly around Bristol and stretching westwards to Cardiff. During this period, the UK was part of the supercontinent Pangea. It was located far closer to the equator, at a latitude of around 20–30°N, around the modern-day location of Niger and Chad. Its arid climate meant that fewer fossils from this period were preserved.

In the subsequent Jurassic period (208–146 million years ago), Pangea was breaking up and the UK was drifting northwards. Much of the UK was covered by shallow seas and floodplains – ideal conditions for fossil making. Dinosaur fossils from this period can be found bisecting Middle England, from Peterborough through to Oxford, and down to Dorset.

As the UK neared its modern-day position during the Cretaceous period (146–65 million years ago), many fossils were formed in the south-eastern corner of England, across Sussex and Hampshire.

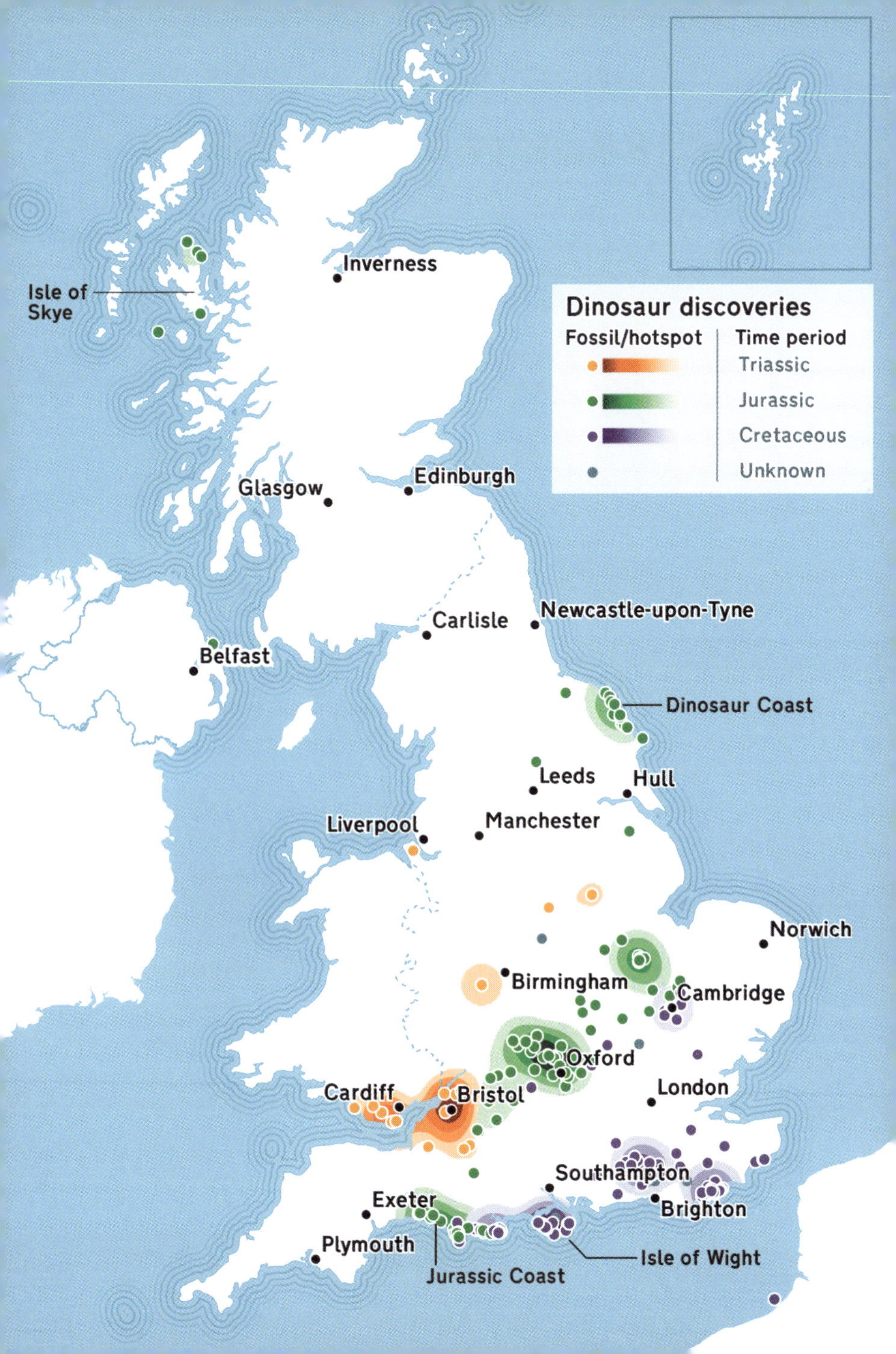

Dinosaur discoveries
Fossil/hotspot
Time period
Triassic
Jurassic
Cretaceous
Unknown
Inverness
Isle of Skye
Glasgow
Edinburgh
Belfast
Carlisle
Newcastle-upon-Tyne
Dinosaur Coast
Leeds
Hull
Liverpool
Manchester
Norwich
Birmingham
Cambridge
Oxford
Cardiff
Bristol
London
Southampton
Brighton
Exeter
Plymouth
Isle of Wight
Jurassic Coast

Red squirrel sightings

Of all of Britain's wildlife, there are few animals as beloved as the red squirrel. Their grey counterparts were originally introduced as ornamental pets and curiosities to the grounds of stately homes, and it wasn't until 1930 that it became illegal to release them into the wild, but by then the damage was done. Greys carry squirrel pox, which is fatal to reds, and they are also prolific breeders. Consequently, red squirrel populations in Britain have been severely affected. Once thought to number around 3.5 million, the Woodland Trust now estimates red squirrel numbers to be as low as 160,000 individuals.

If you're keen to spot one of these iconic animals, head north. Of the 60,700 sightings between 2019 and 2023, 96 per cent have been in Scotland, with appearances relatively common in the lowland belt between Aberdeen and Glasgow.

A further 3 per cent of sightings have been in Northern Ireland, which is fairly high when you consider Scotland is nearly six times larger.

Sightings in England and Wales remain far more rare and limited to isolated locations. In the north, these areas include Formby Red Squirrel Reserve, across the Lake District (particularly around Aira Force, Allan Bank and Grasmere) and Northumberland. Further south, red squirrels become even more isolated, and can mostly be found on islands – such as the Isle of Wight and Dorset's Brownsea Island – where their grey counterparts never reached.

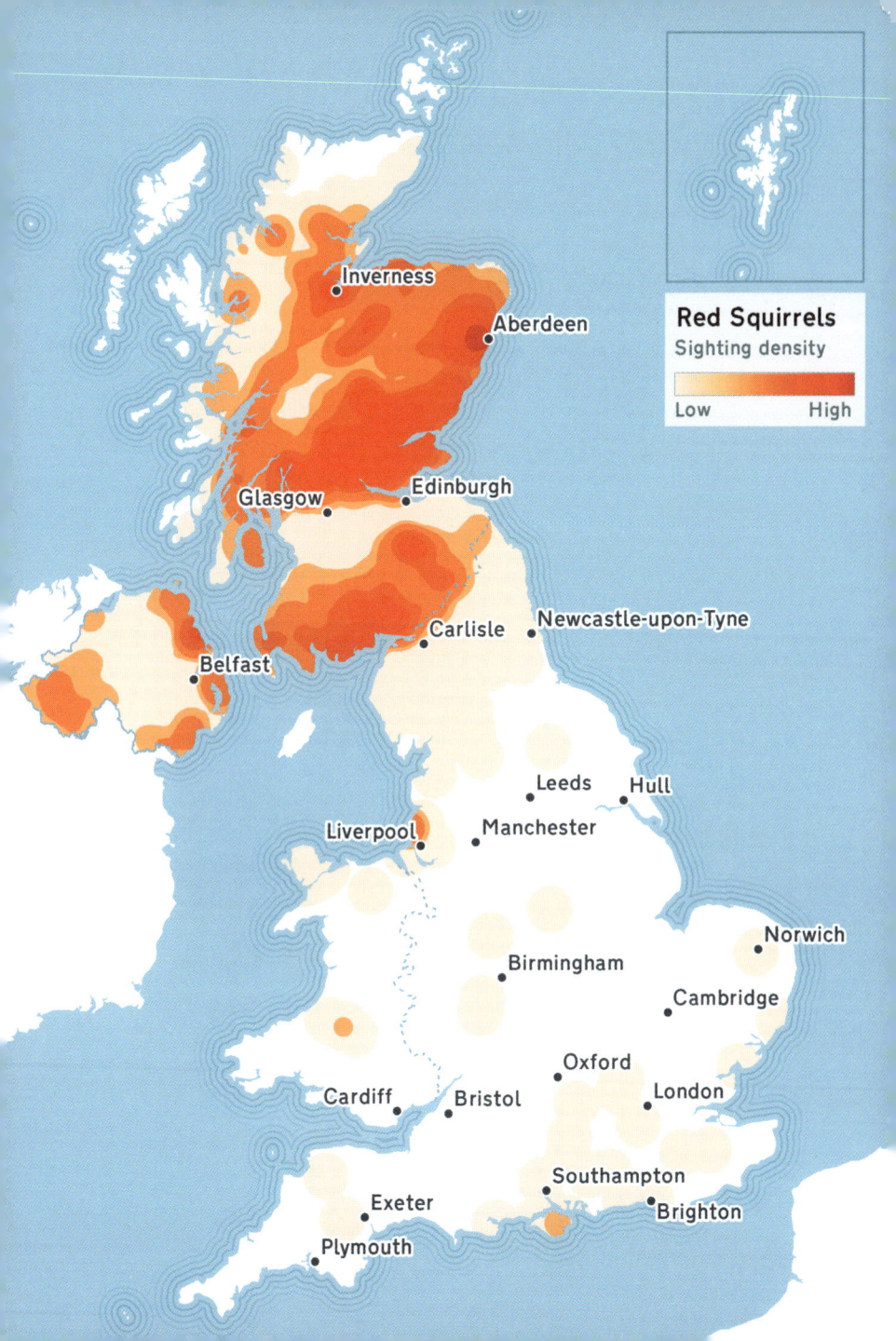

Red Squirrels
Sighting density

Low — High

Red kite recovery

Red kites are one of the great success stories in UK conservation.

Once a common sight – even in cities – their population saw extreme decline from the 15th century onwards, due to being seen as vermin, with King James II of Scotland stating they should be 'killed wherever possible'. However, despite their size and public image, they actually lack the strength to carry off larger animals like chickens and household pets. Their reputation for kleptomania, meanwhile, is well deserved. Red kites have been recorded stealing everything from handbags and crisp packets to tea towels and underwear. They were even referenced in Shakespeare's *The Winter's Tale*; 'when the kite builds, look to your lesser linen'.

A re-introduction programme was launched in 1989. During this time, red kites from Europe were introduced across the UK, including in Wales, Dumfries and Galloway, the Derwent Valley and throughout the south-east of England. Thanks to these conservation efforts, the British red kite population has soared by 2,232 per cent between 1995 and 2022, according to the RSPB. In these maps, you can see how their distribution has changed in the last 30 years, from isolated populations, to becoming a widespread species. They can now even be spotted in urban areas like London and Newcastle.

These maps are based on sightings data from the RSPB, Argyll Biological Records Centre and Birda.

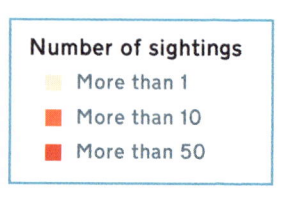

Number of sightings
More than 1
More than 10
More than 50

1990

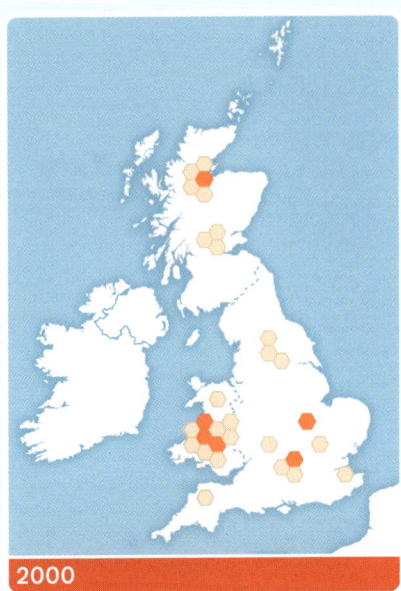

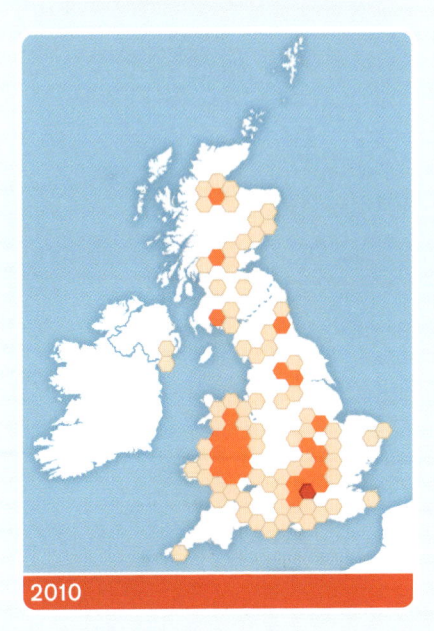

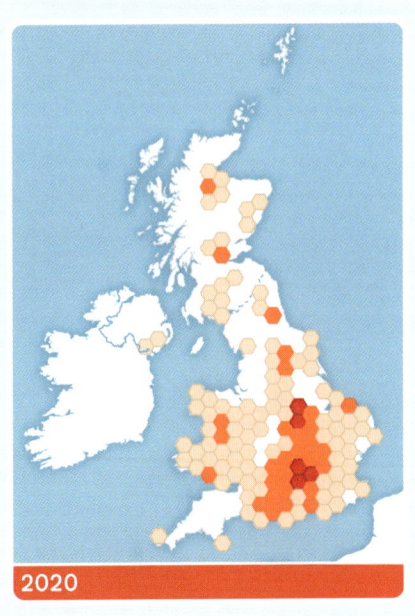

2000

2010

2020

75

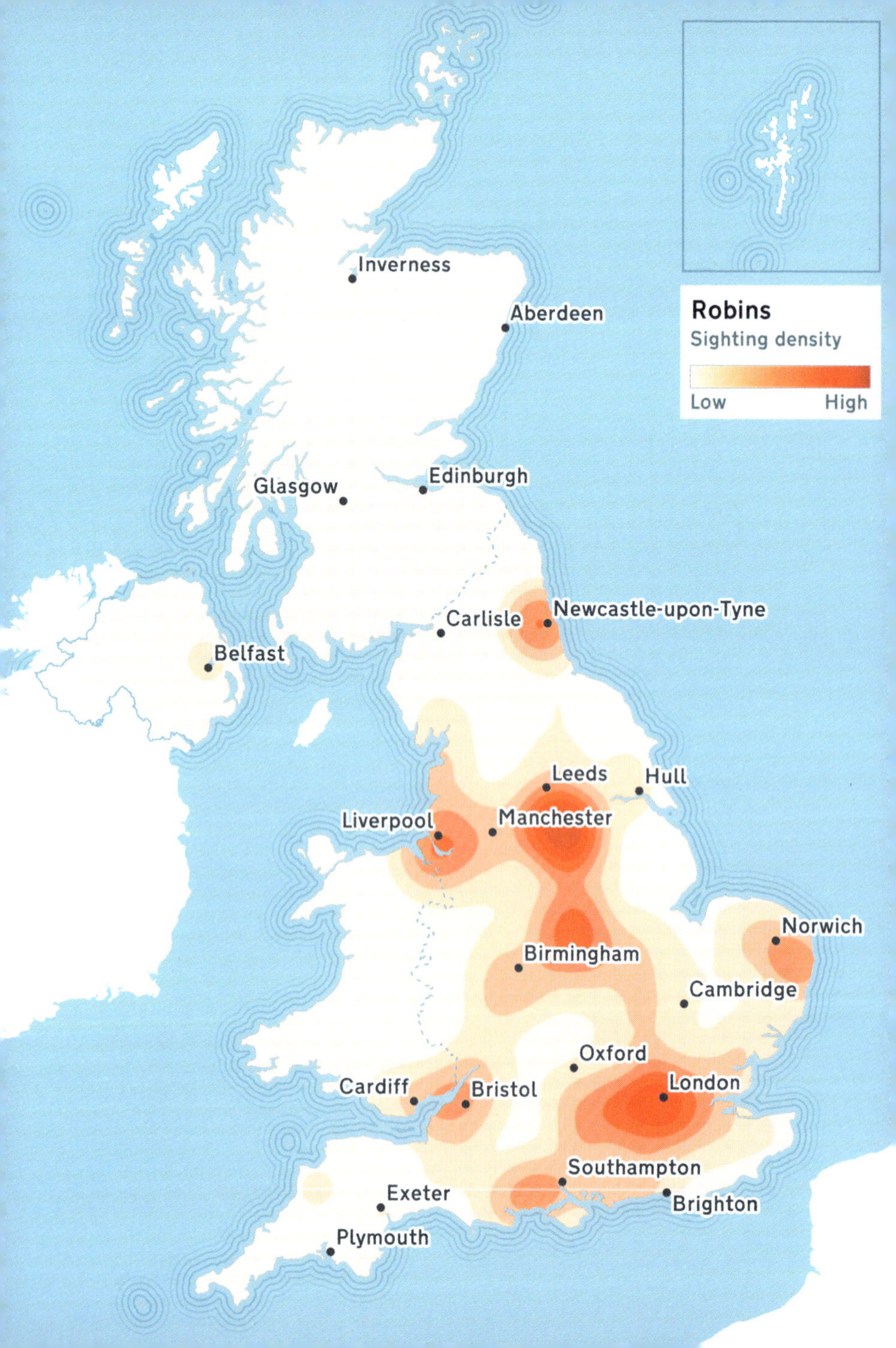

Robin hotspots

The robin is the official national bird of the United Kingdom. In a 2015 poll of 224,000 people by The Urban Birder, David Lindo, 34 per cent voted the robin as their favourite bird, flying leagues ahead of the runners-up – the barn owl (12 per cent) and the blackbird (11 per cent). Seagulls somehow did not make the top ten. Our love of the cheeky redbreast is no fickle thing. In 1961, the robin also topped a poll for the UK's favourite bird conducted by the International Council for Bird Preservation.

As this map of sightings in 2023 shows, robins are incredibly common across the UK, with 17,000 reported sightings – and of course many thousands more unreported. They're also extremely widespread, with sightings across the whole country. The only exceptions to this are the Outer Hebrides and Shetland Islands, where any robin you see is more likely to be a Scandinavian – rather than British – robin.

Sightings of robins are also common in urban environments – even in large conurbations like London and Manchester. While there is some correlation between sightings and population density, robins are known for being a garden bird, and thriving in coexistence with people. Their red chest, white belly and popularity on Christmas cards makes them very easy to identify in comparison with many other garden birds. They are also very likely to approach people, not necessarily due to friendliness, but due to their territorial nature – what seems like a chatty encounter is probably just them telling you to get off their land.

Top four garden birds

When you think about birdwatching, you probably imagine having to get up at the crack of dawn – binoculars in one hand, various rain-repelling gear in the other – to venture to some remote corner of the countryside. However, birdwatching is actually something you can do by opening your back door, with a cup of freshly brewed tea.

Every year since 1979, the Royal Society for the Protection of Birds (RSPB) has facilitated a Big Garden Birdwatch to build a picture of local bird populations. In 2024, over 600,000 people took part across one weekend – counting a massive 9.7 million birds!

So what did they see? The cheerful house sparrow was by far the most common bird, with over 1.4 million sightings. The sparrow is extremely widespread, being the most common bird across all corners of the UK. In second place was the blue tit, with more than 900,000 sightings, and was particularly common across the south-east of England. In third place was the starling, again with around 900,000 sightings, and was the most common bird in parts of Northern Ireland and some of the Scottish islands.

This form of citizen science is crucial. While it may seem like the UK is teeming with birdlife (particularly if you've ever tried to eat fish and chips on Brighton beach), the RSPB actually estimates that we've lost around 38 million birds from our skies in the last 60 years. Even the hardy house sparrow – our most common garden bird – has seen its population decline by 60 per cent since the survey began.

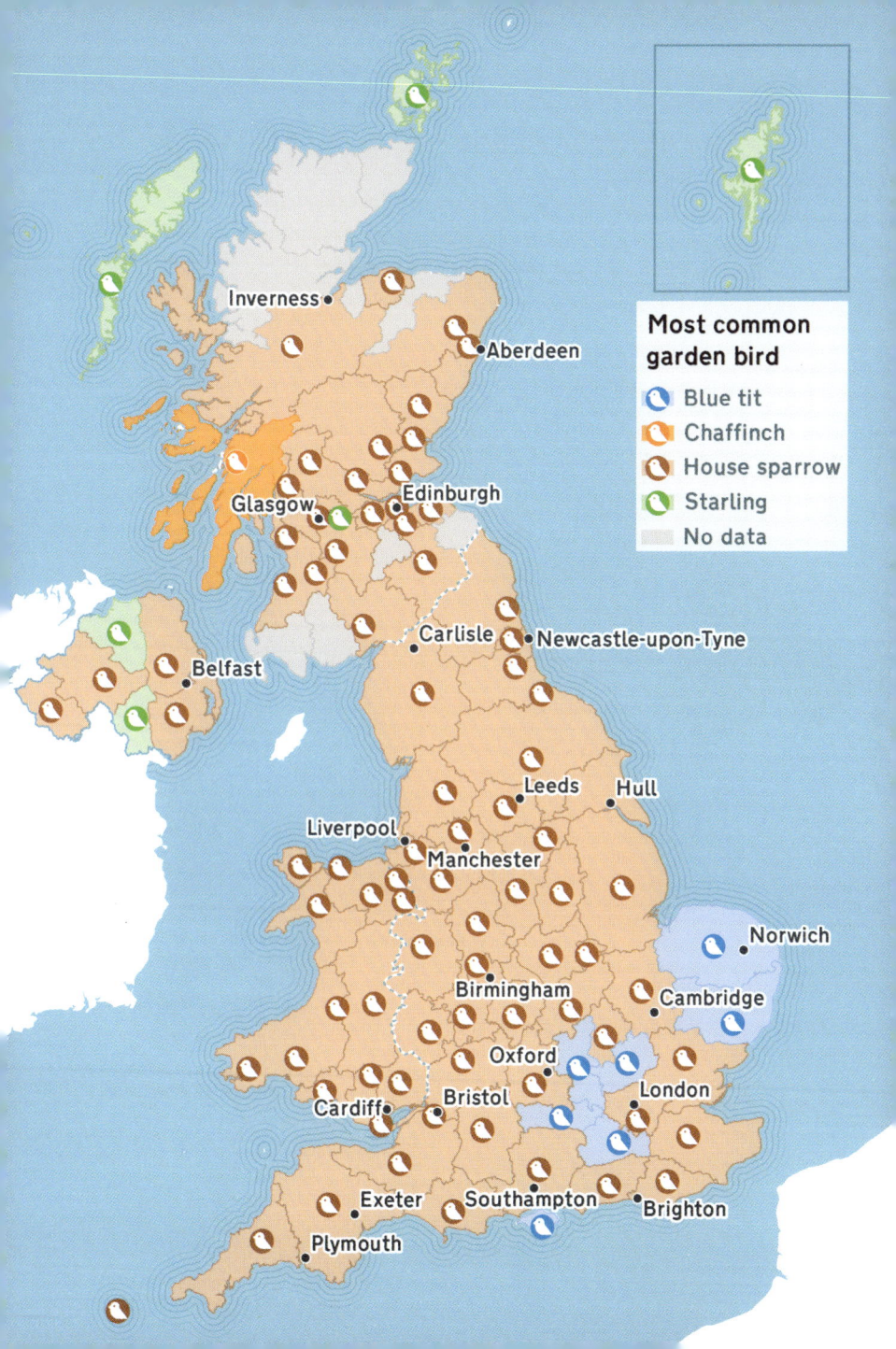

Most common garden bird
- Blue tit
- Chaffinch
- House sparrow
- Starling
- No data

Cattle

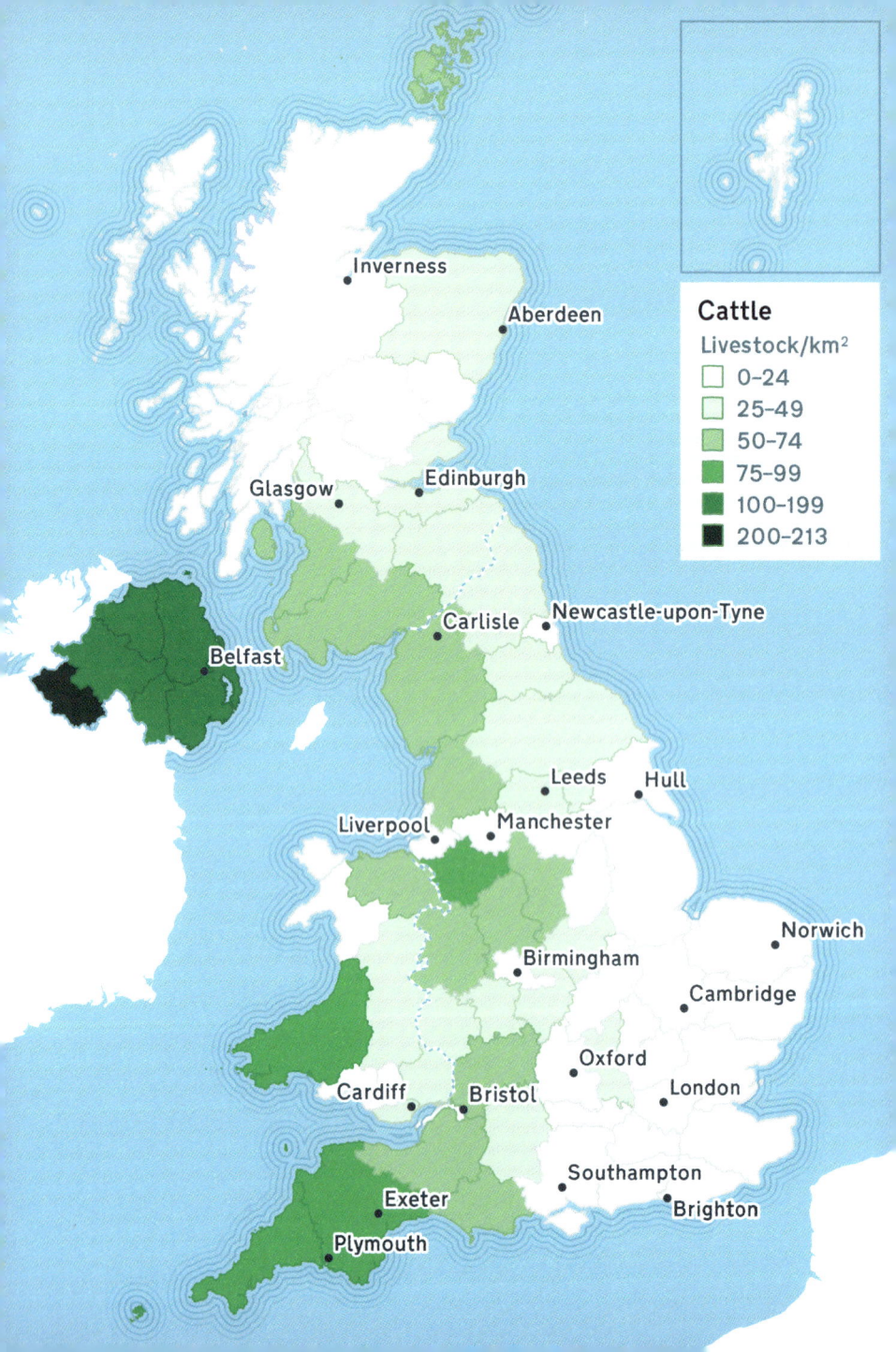

Livestock/km²

- 0–24
- 25–49
- 50–74
- 75–99
- 100–199
- 200–213

British farm animals

The UK boasts a massive 16.8 million hectares (41.5 million acres) of farmland, covering about 69 per cent of our total land according to the Department for Environment Food and Rural Affairs. A large majority of this land is given over to livestock – as well as the production of food for the animals. This consists of land for 176 million poultry, 9.4 million cows, 14.9 million sheep and lambs, 4.7 million pigs and just one partridge in a pear tree.

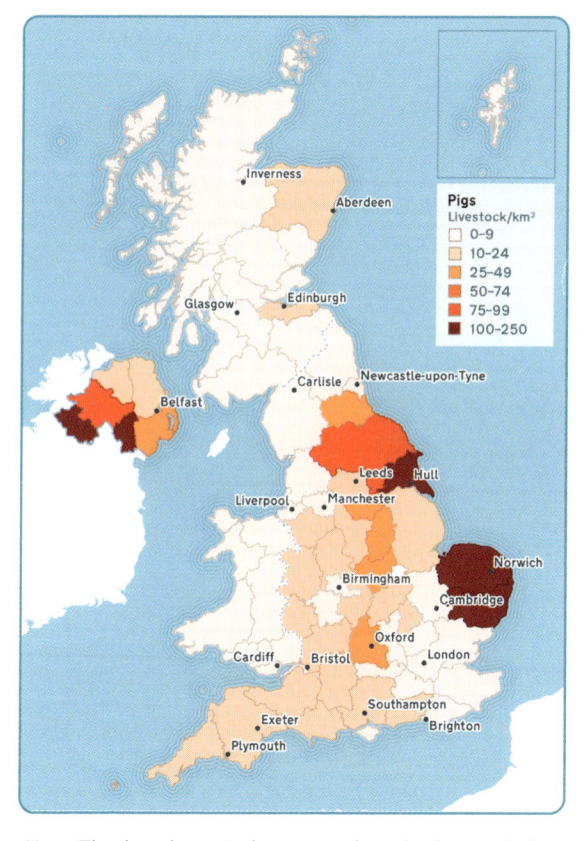

Note: The data shown in these maps shows land set aside for livestock per km² (0.4 sq. mile).

There's a real geography to where these animals live. In general, the farming of livestock is more common towards the west of the UK. This is because the low-lying, fertile loam soils and relatively warm climate make the east more suited to arable crop farming.

In rugged upland areas – like parts of Wales and Scotland – you're more likely to see sheep and goats. They're much better adapted to these areas than other farmland animals due to their woolly coats, hardy nature and mountaineering aptitude.

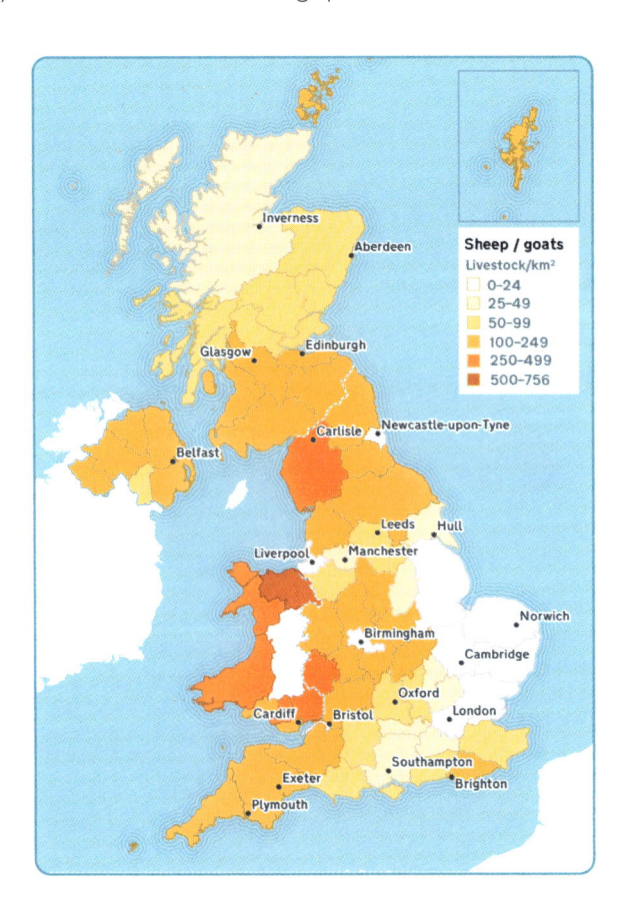

Cattle demand a huge amount of lush grass to keep their four stomachs churning. They thrive in the rainy yet fertile lands of Northern Ireland and England's South West.

Pig farming is a popular occupation in East Anglia – due to the soil being perfect for producing pig food such as barley and wheat – and across Yorkshire, a region which has a proud heritage of pig farming.

Chickens, on the other hand, will live anywhere.

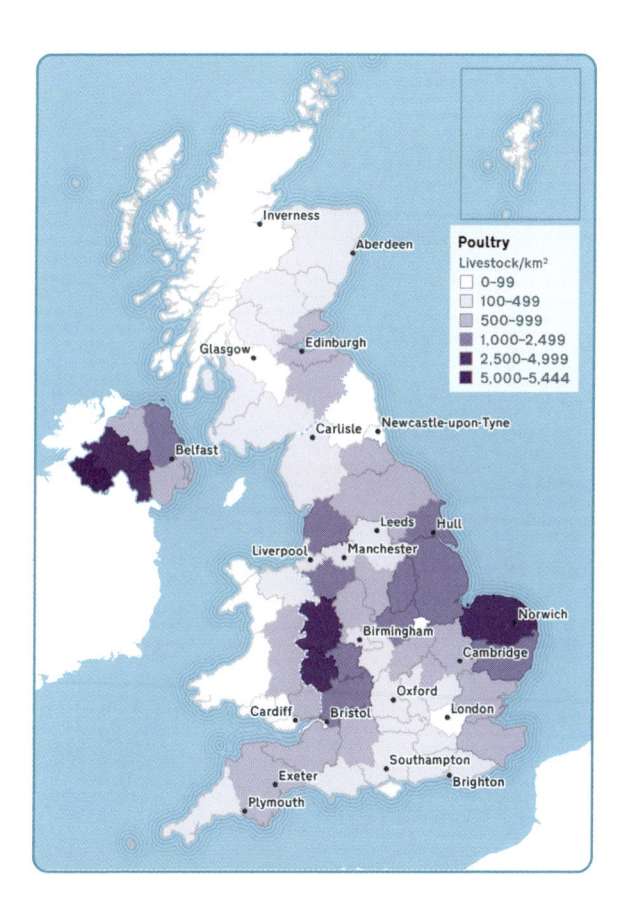

Weather

Rainy days and sunny spells –
our favourite conversation, mapped

Polar Maritime
❄ **Wet, cold air for cold, rainy weather**

Returning Polar Maritime
☀ **Moist, mild & unstable air brings cloud & rain**

Why our weather is so unpredictable

If there's one thing all Brits have in common, it's our ability to wax lyrical about our weather. This is probably because the UK has a relatively varied climate – in large part due to the air masses that make their way over to our little island from across the globe. There's damp air from the Atlantic bringing rain, fighting off dry air from mainland Europe. There's cold weather blowing in from the north, versus warmer air from the south. This – along with the UK's topography – makes for some really interesting regional and local weather patterns, which we'll be exploring in this chapter.

Arctic Maritime
🌡 ❄ Cold, wet air for snowy winters

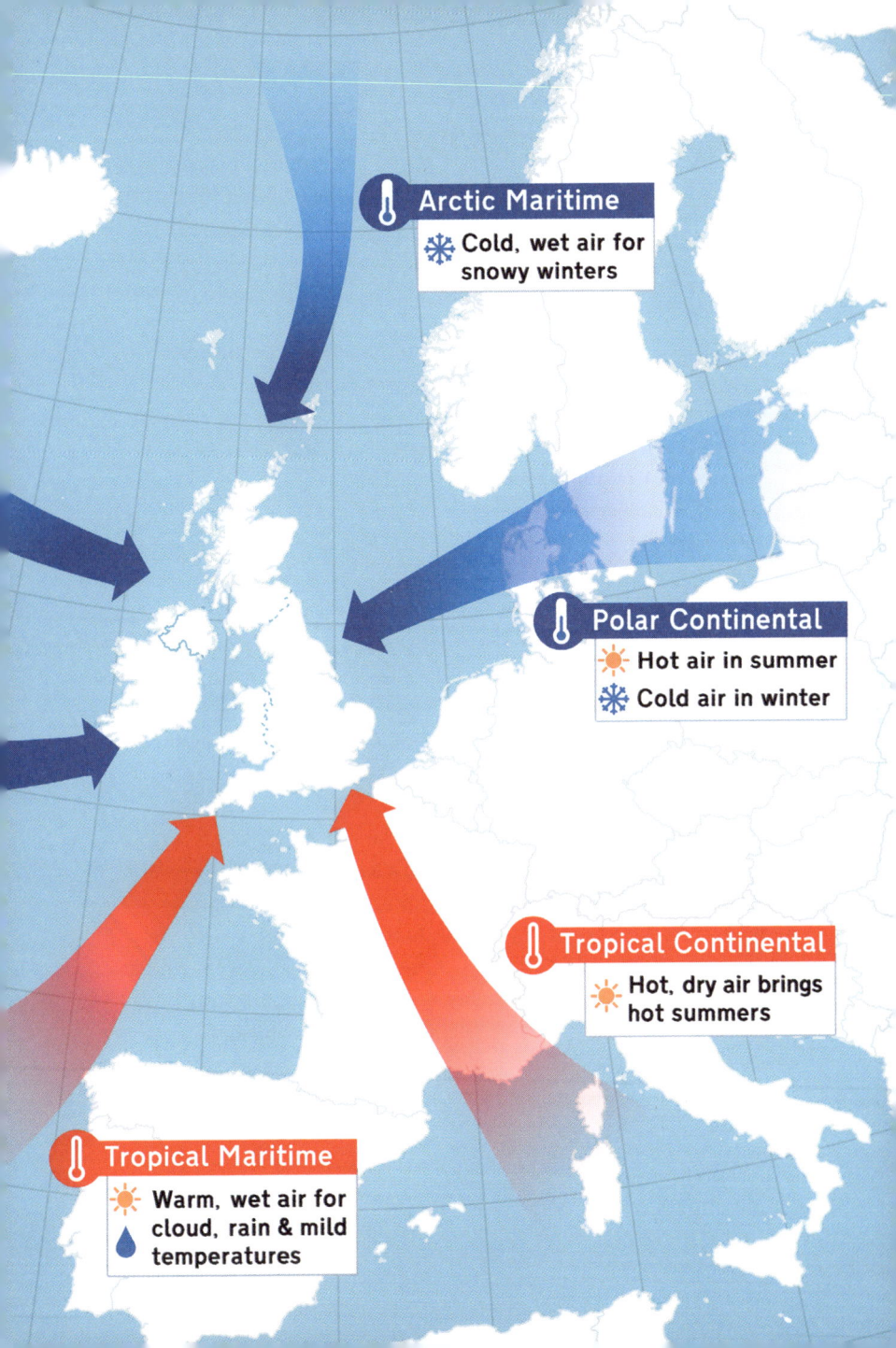

Polar Continental
🌡 ☀ Hot air in summer
❄ Cold air in winter

Tropical Continental
🌡 ☀ Hot, dry air brings hot summers

Tropical Maritime
🌡 ☀ Warm, wet air for cloud, rain & mild temperatures 💧

Microclimates

While it can be easy to think of the UK as covered by the same sort of grey, mizzly blanket of cloud day-in, day-out, we actually experience an awful lot of weather variation for such a small country.

Roughly, the country can be divided into four main climate zones. The north tends to experience cooler summers than the south – which will come as no surprise to anyone who's attempted a summer holiday in the Outer Hebrides. Meanwhile, the west fares better in winter with a generally milder climate. This means that if you're looking for the most pleasant year-round weather, you'd better head to the South West – but don't expect idyllic snowy winter days.

There are, of course, variations within these zones. Warmer pockets of the UK include the South West peninsula – mostly driven by the majority of the landmass being in close proximity to the sea – which experiences less seasonal variation in temperature compared inland. Then there's the urban heat island of London – at its centre, temperatures can be up to 10°C warmer than surrounding counties.

At the other end of the country, there's the notably colder climate of the Highlands and Shetland Islands. This is caused by the region's high latitude and altitude, as well as exposure to strong winds and weather systems blowing in from the Arctic and Atlantic. However, the western coast and Shetland Islands are slightly milder than areas of a similar latitude, such as southern Greenland and Norway. This is due to the influence of the Gulf Stream – the warm ocean current which originates near Mexico and the Caribbean.

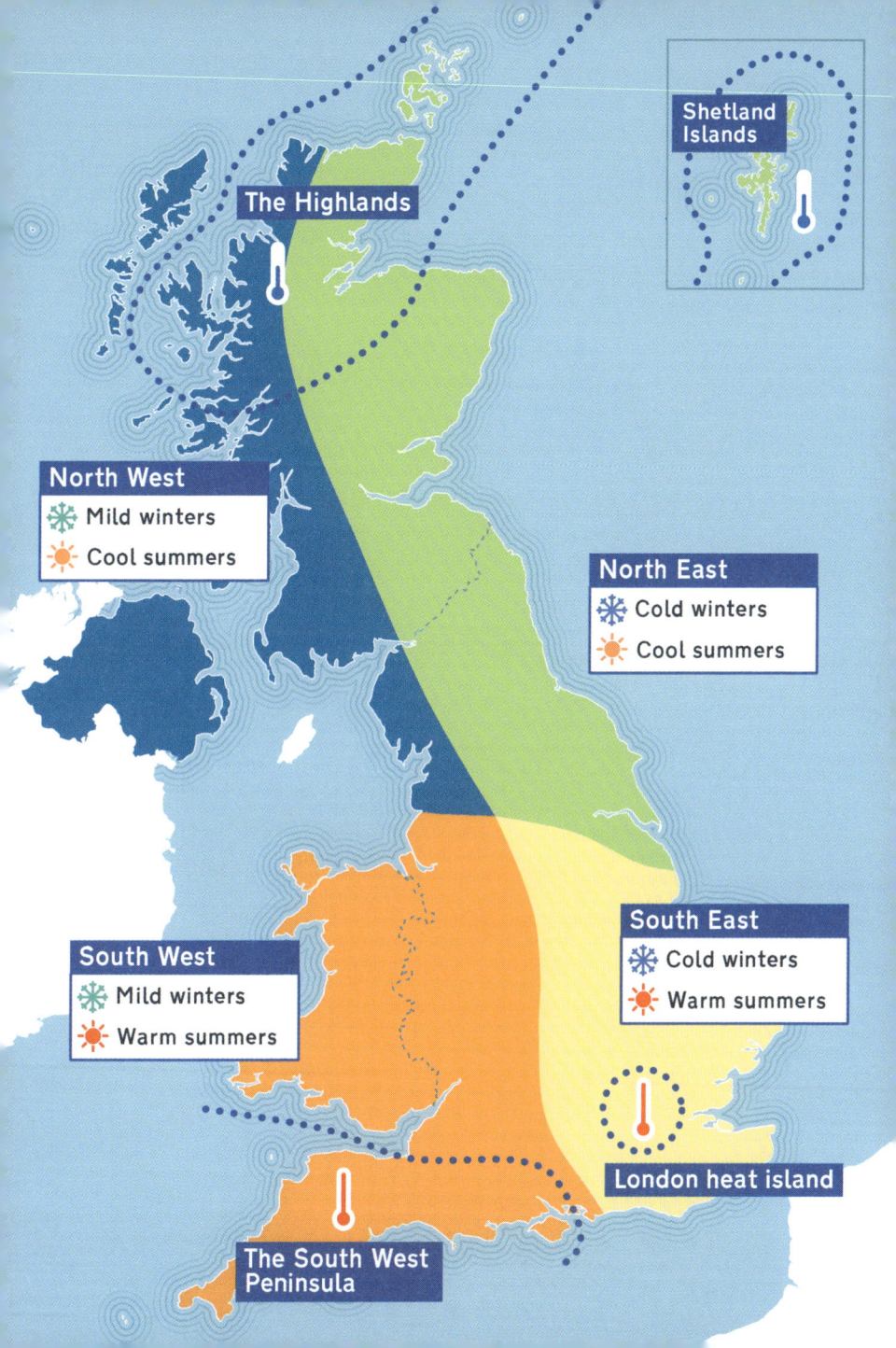

The Highlands

Shetland Islands

North West
- ❄ Mild winters
- ☀ Cool summers

North East
- ❄ Cold winters
- ☀ Cool summers

South West
- ❄ Mild winters
- ☀ Warm summers

South East
- ❄ Cold winters
- ☀ Warm summers

London heat island

The South West Peninsula

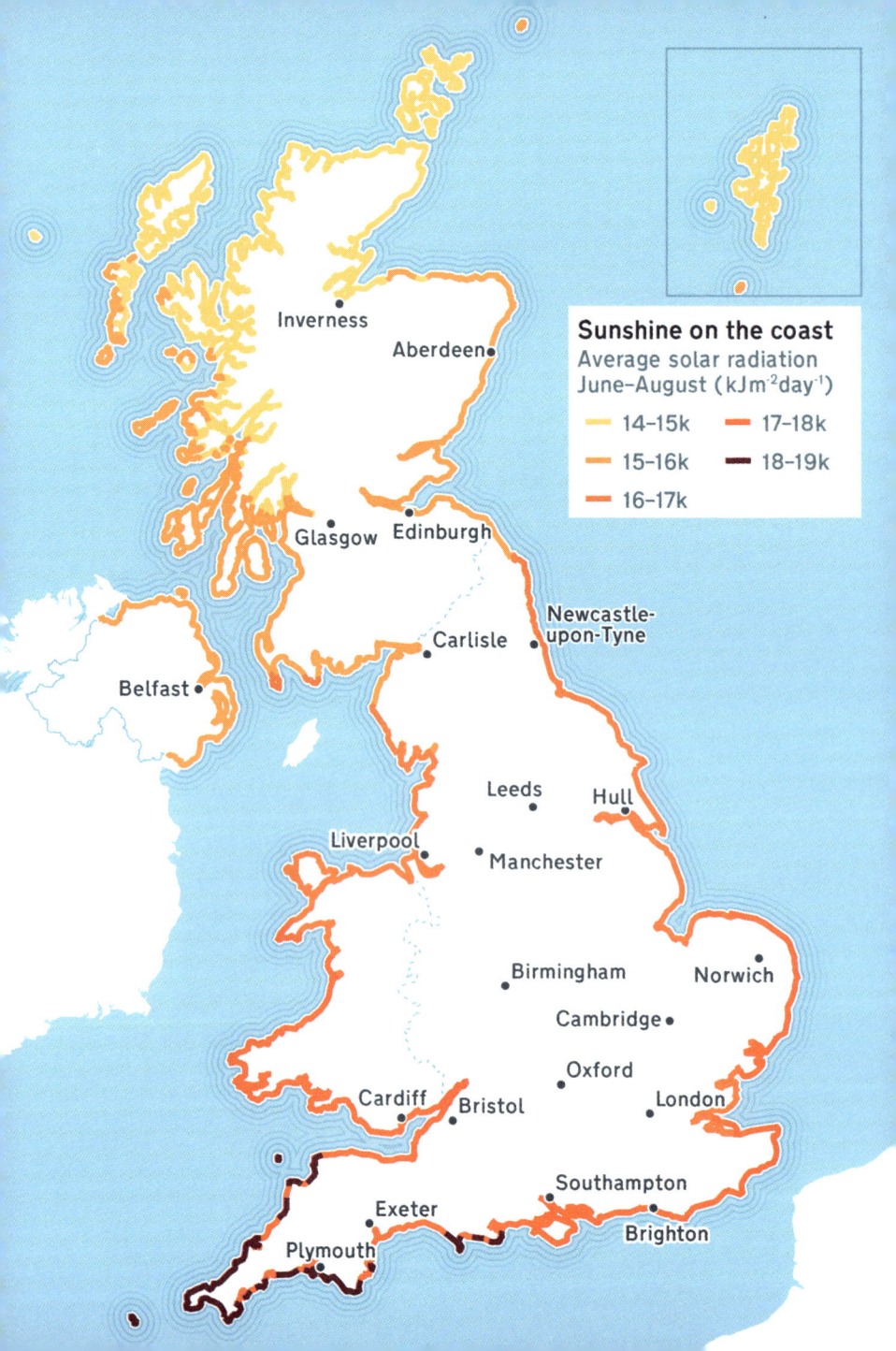

Sunshine on the coast
Average solar radiation
June–August (kJm^{-2}day^{-1})

- 14–15k
- 15–16k
- 16–17k
- 17–18k
- 18–19k

Sunniest beaches

Looking to top up your tan at the beach? The South West is your best bet, with this region experiencing by far the strongest sun in the country – particularly during the summer months. The most sunshine can be found on the exposed beaches dotted around major headlands, like Devon's south coast, and beaches near Cornwall's Padstow and Land's End.

However, it's the Lizard Peninsula in Cornwall that hosts some of the sunniest beaches – no surprises there, as it's also the most southerly part of the country. However, it's also a very rugged landscape with steep cliffs, crashing waves and a thriving fishing industry. Some of these beaches double up as harbours, and to reach them you may be better off packing hiking boots – or even abseiling gear – than your flip-flops and SPF 30.

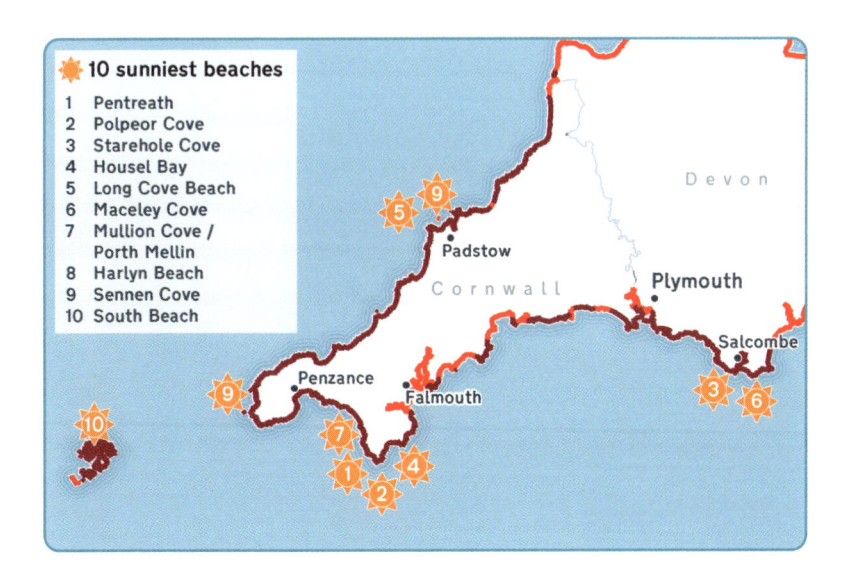

10 sunniest beaches
1. Pentreath
2. Polpeor Cove
3. Starehole Cove
4. Housel Bay
5. Long Cove Beach
6. Maceley Cove
7. Mullion Cove / Porth Mellin
8. Harlyn Beach
9. Sennen Cove
10. South Beach

Rainiest places

The UK has a reputation for grey skies and damp days, and in fact we've made talking (or, perhaps, complaining) about it a national pastime. But you'll rarely hear a Brit simply say, 'It's raining.' It'll be spitting, tipping, bucketing or chucking it down. It might be raining cats and dogs, coming in stair rods or simply a nice day for ducks. There are estimated to be between 50 and 100 words for rain, from common phrases to regional terms; while it may be 'plothering' in the Midlands, it's more likely to be 'stoating' in Scotland.

Despite the UK's mizzly image, we are actually only the 74th rainiest country in the world. Fiji, Granada and the Seychelles all trump us when it comes to rainfall, but you never hear of anyone mocking their weather.

We experience around 1,200mm (47.2in) of rainfall on average per year. The rainiest parts of the UK can be found to the north and west, particularly in areas exposed to the incoming (supposedly) warm moist air blowing over from the Atlantic Ocean, which is particularly damp, with Argyll and Bute, Inverness, and Ross and Cromarty seeing the most rain. Northern Ireland slightly bucks this trend due to the wet prevailing winds breaking on the high terrain of Ireland's eastern coast.

At the other end of the scale, it's south-east England which is the driest part of the UK. The driest area of all is Cambridgeshire; its latitude and inland position mean it experiences less than half of the UK's average annual rainfall, and around one-fifth of that which 'stoats' down on Argyll and Bute.

Annual average rainfall by county

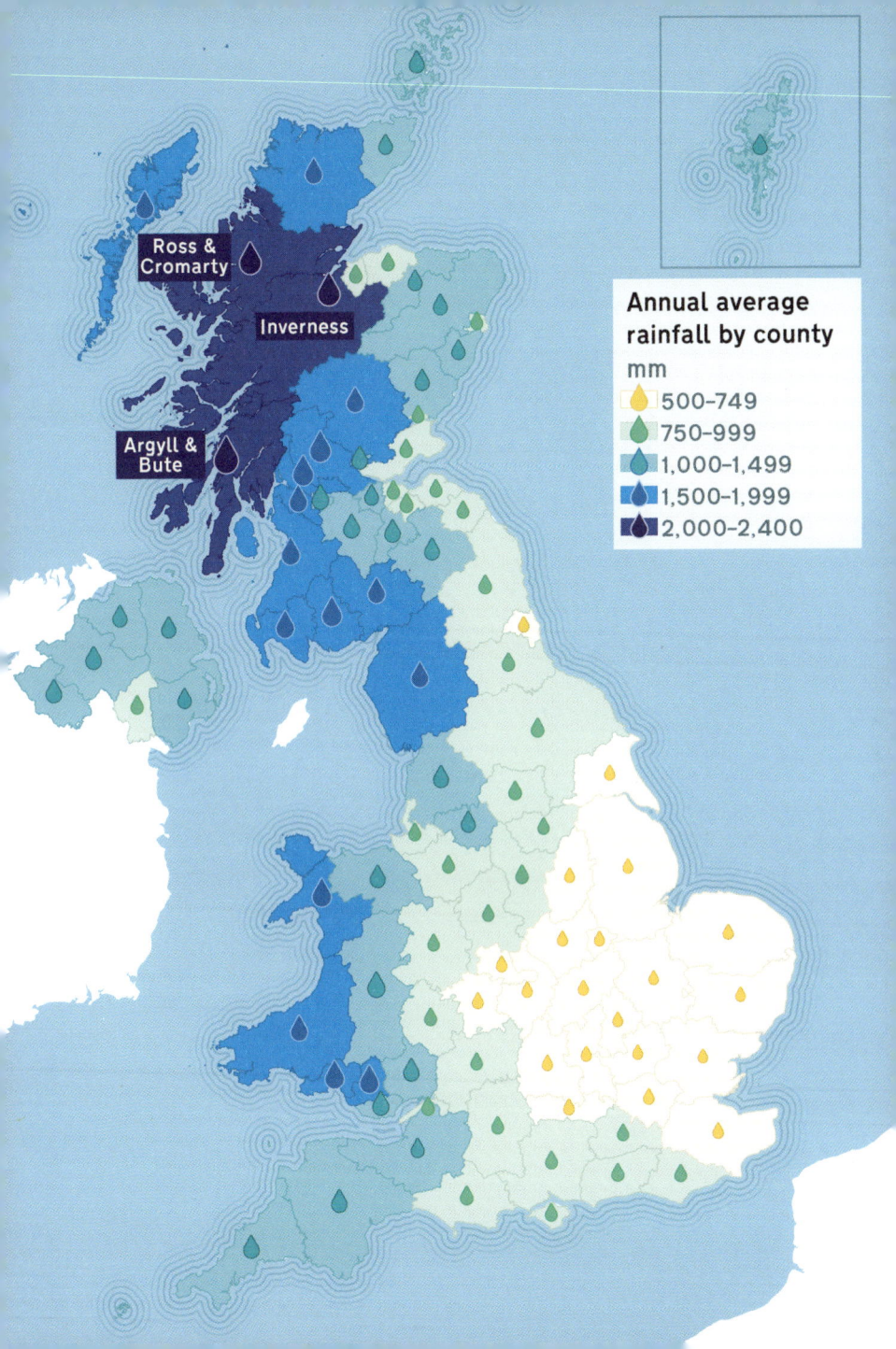

mm
- 500–749
- 750–999
- 1,000–1,499
- 1,500–1,999
- 2,000–2,400

Ross & Cromarty
Inverness
Argyll & Bute

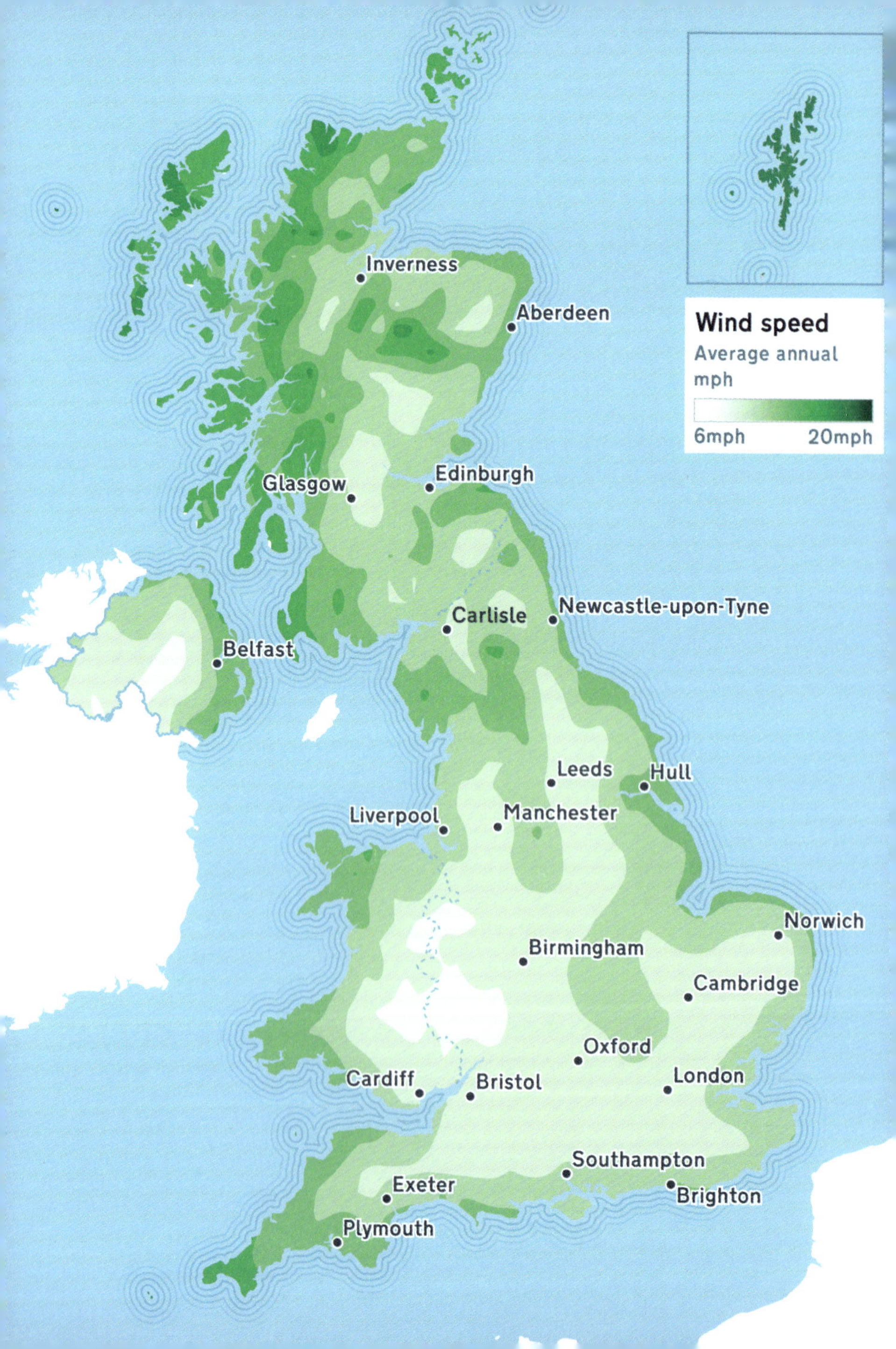

Windiest areas

Tucked in the north-eastern corner of the second biggest ocean on Earth, the UK is subject to gusts and gales galore.

The average wind speed across the UK is around 16kph (10mph – or roughly 8.9 knots, if you're more of a 'knots' person). High winds are more typical around the coast – particularly on the Atlantic-facing west – and exposed islands, like the Shetland Islands and Outer Hebrides. Upland areas – like the Scottish Highlands, Lake District and Pennines – also face bigger gales. These wind-battered areas do a great job of sheltering the rest of the country, with inland and lowland areas generally experiencing gentler winds – the lowest around the Anglo-Welsh border and central Northern Ireland.

This map shows average annual wind speeds, but storms can bring far, far stronger gusts. The highest recorded wind speed was in 1986 at the summit of Cairn Gorm in the Scottish Highlands. Winds were recorded up to 278kph (173mph) – equivalent to a Category 5 hurricane!

While we often associate wind with negatives – blown over trees, inside-out umbrellas and terrible hair days – there are a lot of positives to being a breezy country. The UK is – for example – a world leader in green energy production from wind. We have over 11,000 wind turbines, generating over 82 terawatts of power annually, which according to the Department for Energy Security and Net Zero accounts for roughly 30 per cent of our energy. Other benefits of a gusty day include air pollution dispersal, water supply oxygenation and the breaking up of algal blooms.

Chance of a white Christmas

Dreaming of a white Christmas? According to the UK Met Office, there is only a 1 in 4 chance you'll see snow on the ground on Christmas Day. However, in some parts of the country your white Christmas fantasy is far more likely to come true.

Generally, for those iconic Christmas morning scenes you'll want to head north and to higher ground, with Scotland – and the Scottish Highlands in particular – being your best bet. The area around Blackwater Reservoir near Kinlochleven in the Scottish Highlands is the snowiest location, with snow on the ground there every year for the last 20 years! In England, the uplands of the Lake District, Pennines and Yorkshire Dales have the highest probability of snow on the ground.

If you live in the south – and particularly the south-east – your chances of a white Christmas are miniscule. Similarly, coastal regions tend to experience less snow. This is because during winter the land is actually cooler than the sea, and the freezing level of the land tends to be closer to the surface in inland areas – meaning snow is more likely to settle. That's why, despite their high latitude, areas like the Shetland Islands and Outer Hebrides actually see far less snow than their inland neighbours.

This means that – for a lot of us – if we're dreaming of a white Christmas, we'd better carry on dreaming.

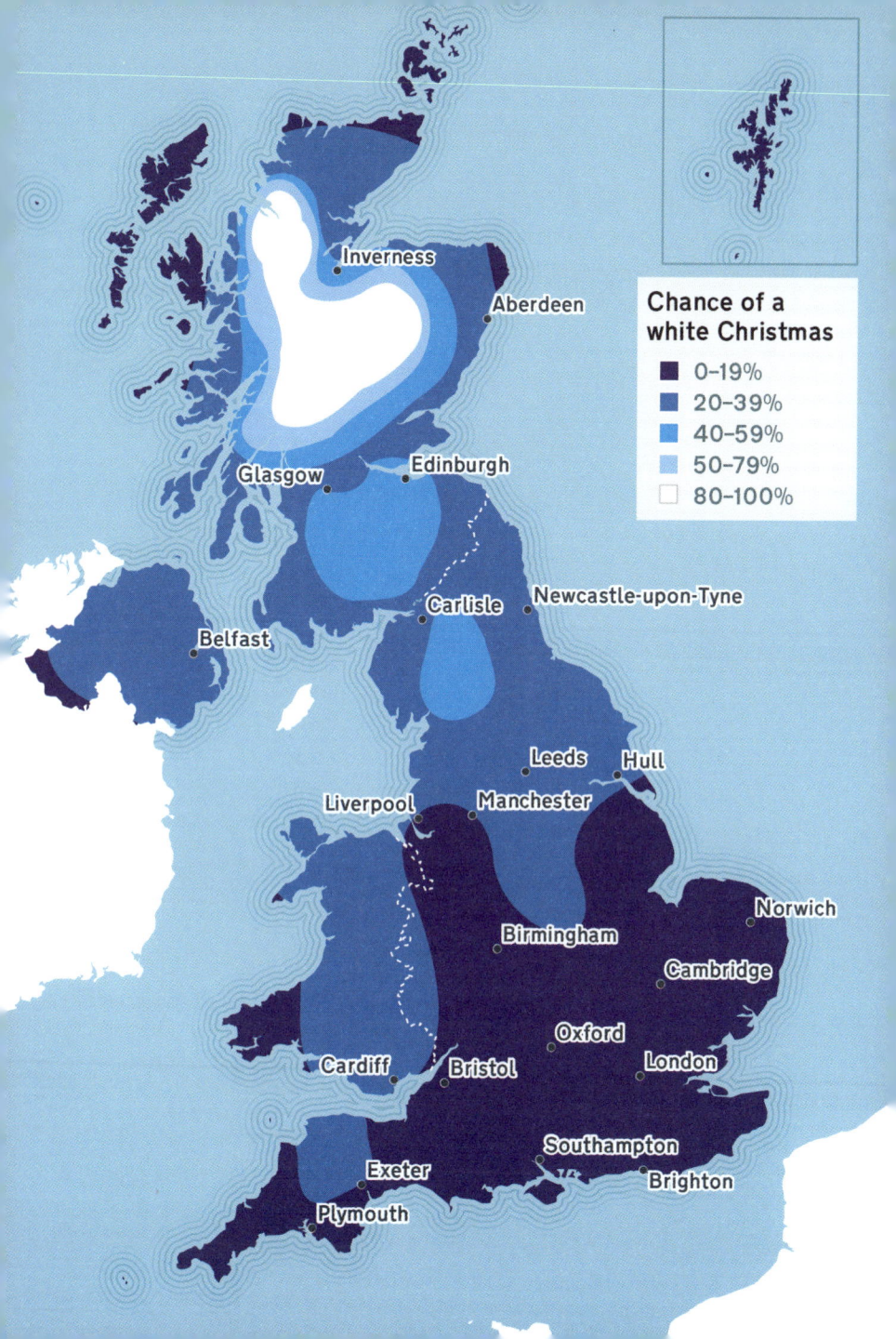

Chance of a white Christmas

- 0–19%
- 20–39%
- 40–59%
- 50–79%
- 80–100%

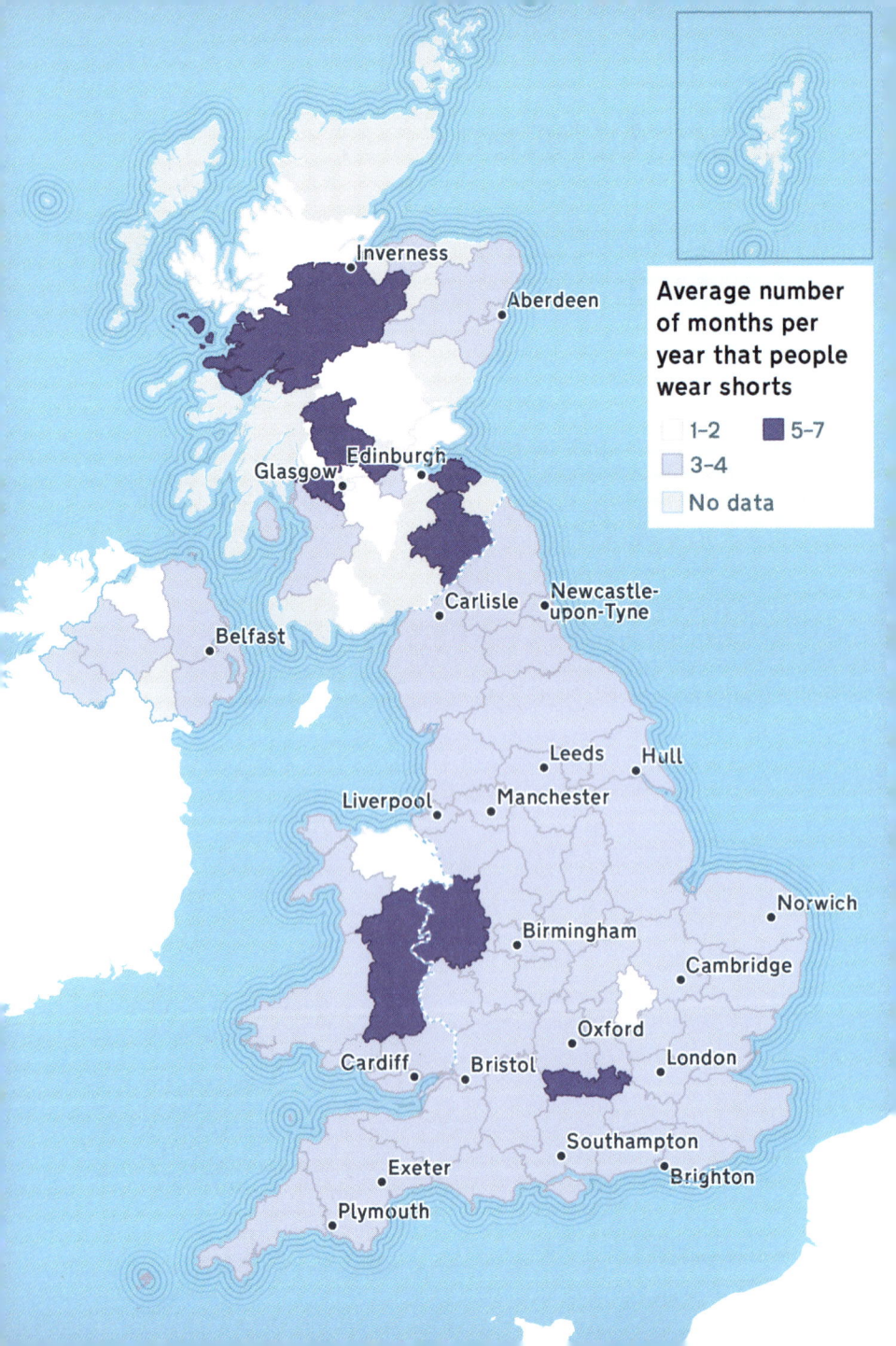

Average number of months per year that people wear shorts

- 1–2
- 3–4
- 5–7
- No data

Shorts weather

The English language is known for – in Britain at least – being jam-packed full of idioms, and this is particularly true when we're talking about the weather. 'Nice weather for ducks' means the day is damp, 'blowing a hoolie' means it's stormy (at least in Scotland), and 'brass monkeys' means it's cold enough to freeze off a particularly colourful part of a monkey's anatomy.

One of the more literal phrases used is 'shorts weather'. This is typically used in the early days of summer, when Brits debate whether the days are becoming warm enough to free their knobbly knees, and graduate from trousers to shorts.

There is some debate as to what shorts weather constitutes. For the majority of Brits, this is the three to four months of the summer period (the end of May to the beginning of September). Interestingly, the further north you travel, the more opinion diverges. In Scotland, where the weather tends to be cooler, some opt for trousers for much of the year, while other brave souls cling to their shorts well into autumn.

Transport

There and back again –
maps of the UK on the move

How motorways are named

When you're traversing the UK's approximately 2,300 miles (3,000km) of motorway, you may be too busy swatting away choruses of 'The Wheels on the Bus' to ponder the question – how did motorways get their names?

The UK's motorway and wider major road network is based on a simple, yet brilliant, naming system: a clock. In England and Wales, these originate from London, with roads divided into six numbered radial zones. These begin with zone 1, through which the A1 races northwards from London, across Hertfordshire, Yorkshire and eventually concluding at Edinburgh.

In Scotland, Edinburgh serves as the centre of the zonal 'clock', with zones radiating clockwise around the Scottish capital. This begins with zone 7, which covers most of south-west Scotland until it spirals round to Glasgow, where zone 8 leads into zone 9.

Like everything in the UK, there are many exceptions to these rules. For example, the M5 connects Birmingham in zone 5 – through zone 4 via Bristol – to Exeter in zone 3. Similarly, the A47 breaks the mould by running from the ever-rebelling Birmingham through zones 5, 6 and 1, where it finishes in Great Yarmouth.

This system does not extend to Northern Ireland, where there is currently no zoning system in place.

Major road number

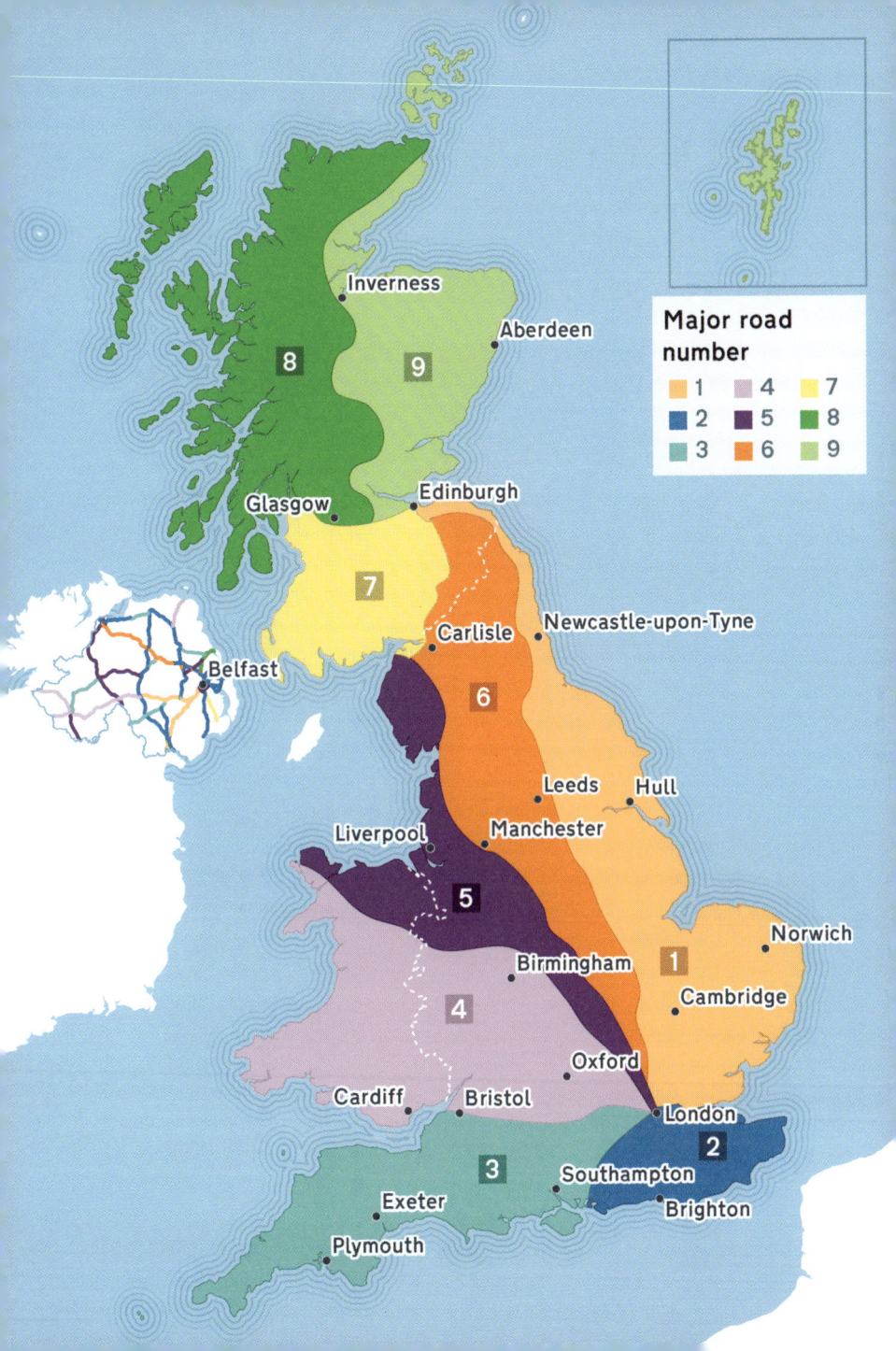

1	4	7
2	5	8
3	6	9

Strange road names

We've already covered the weird and wonderful place names of the UK, but why stop there? There are roughly 262,300 miles (42,200km) of road in the UK and many of them have been given some real head-scratchers for names.

In classic British fashion, many of these are too risqué to include in a family friendly book like this; we'll draw the line at Titty Ho and Spanker Lane, and leave you to fill in the gaps.

There are some that were potentially named just to make postcard-writing an extreme sport. York's Whip-Ma-Whop-Ma-Gate may be the best example of this, its name thought to mean 'neither one thing nor the other' street. Bristol's There and Back Again Lane – thought to be named in honour of J. R. R. Tolkien – is a mere 100ft (30m) long, making it a real challenge for cartographers.

Then there are the road names where the street naming and numbering officer (what a job!) clearly ran out of ideas. Avenue Street and Lane Road are great examples of 'it does what it says on the tin' naming.

Illustrious naming aside, the majority of UK streets have more conventional names. High Street, Station Road, Main Street and Church Road/Street are the most common, but who wants to live there when you can live in Happy Land?

Avenue Street
Dick Place
Muttonhole Road
Ring Rash Road
Barn Slaps
Silly Lane
Whip-Ma-Whop-Ma-Gate
Avenue Street
Pocket Handkerchief Lane
Spanker Lane
Ingle Pingle
Potlicker's Lane
Titty Ho
Crotch Crescent
Lane Road
Butts Lane
Frying Pan Alley
Ticklebelly Alley
There and Back Again Lane
Happy Land
Christmas Pie Avenue
French Ordinary Court
Knick Knack Lane
Tilly Whim Lane
Brandy Hole Lane

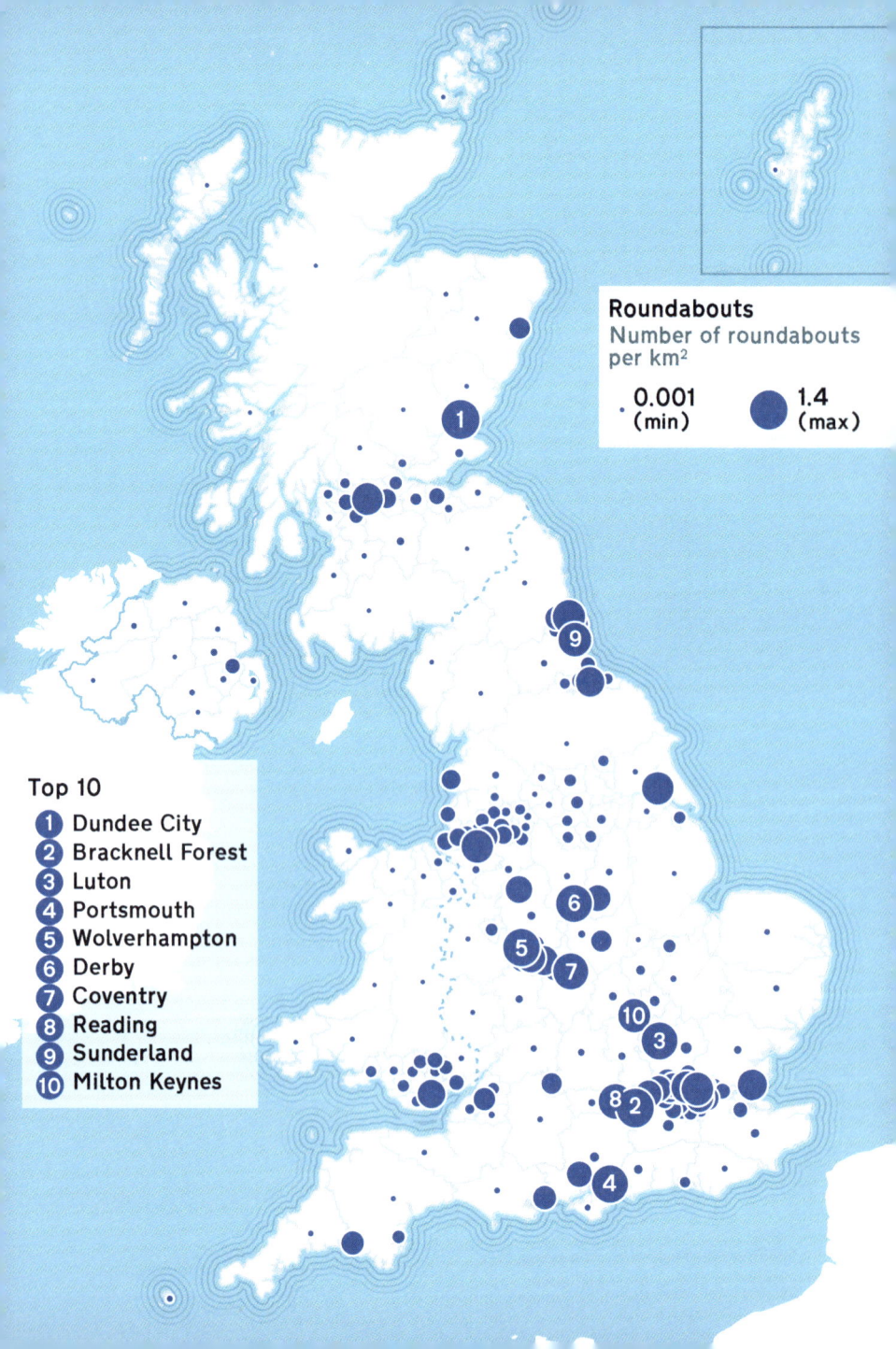

Roundabouts
Number of roundabouts per km²

· 0.001 (min)   ● 1.4 (max)

Top 10
1. Dundee City
2. Bracknell Forest
3. Luton
4. Portsmouth
5. Wolverhampton
6. Derby
7. Coventry
8. Reading
9. Sunderland
10. Milton Keynes

Roundabout hubs

Forget the World Cup and Eurovision, did you know the UK is the roundabout capital of the world? We boast around 25,000 roundabouts, which is roughly one roundabout for every 2,700 people. While Milton Keynes is famed as the 'roundabout capital' of the UK with over 130 roundabouts, they are common across the whole country, with Dundee City having the most roundabouts per km² (0.4 sq. mile).

The most notorious roundabout of all may be Swindon's Magic Roundabout, which consists of five mini-roundabouts that come together to make one super-roundabout.

Other noteworthy roundabouts include Aberdeen's Haudagain Roundabout – the UK's largest roundabout – and the Shepherd and Flock Roundabout in Farnham, Surrey. This has the longest 'circulating lane' in Europe, and is so big it even has a community of residents and a pub marooned on its island!

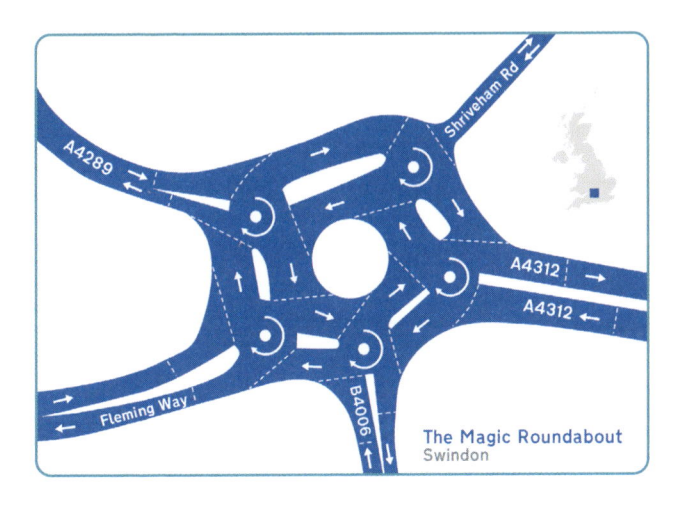

The Magic Roundabout
Swindon

Beautifully complex road junctions

When you picture motorway junctions, you're probably thinking of hours locked in traffic jams as the kids bleat, 'Are we there yet?' at an increasing frequency – and pitch. You probably don't imagine something almost beautiful.

But there is a certain artistry in how the complex road networks curve and interweave, looping over and under each other like the least fun roller-coaster you've ever been on.

Some junctions have a gentle grace, such as the sweeping spirals of the M25 and M3's Thorpe Interchange. Others – like Thorney Junction, bridging the M25 and M24 – have an almost perfect symmetry. And there are those – like the infamous Spaghetti Junction – that seem to have sprung from the worst nightmare of every learner driver in existence.

Here are some of Britain's most beautiful, complicated and – sometimes – frankly baffling motorway junctions.

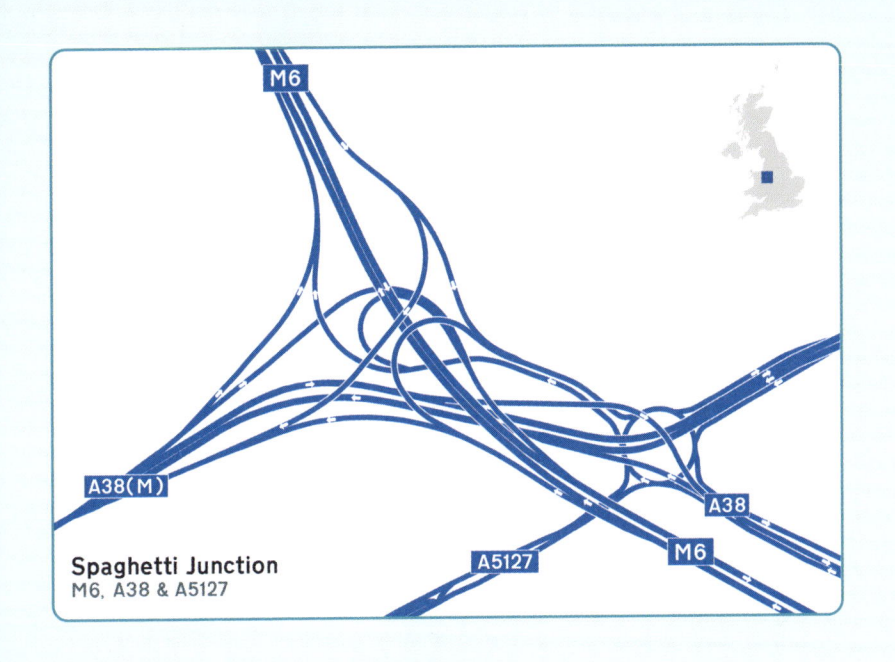

Spaghetti Junction
M6, A38 & A5127

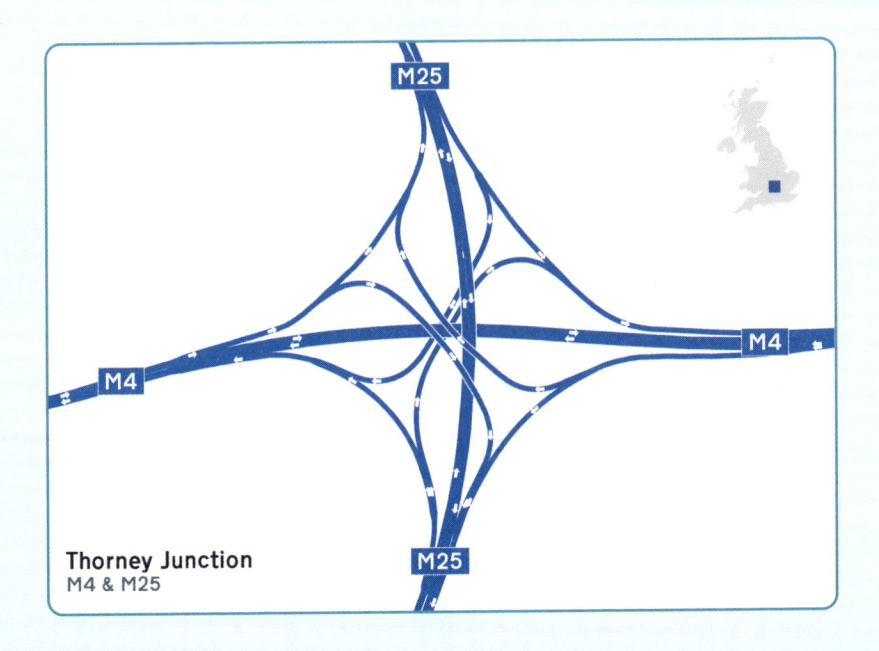

Thorney Junction
M4 & M25

109

Hanger Lane
A40, A406 & A4005

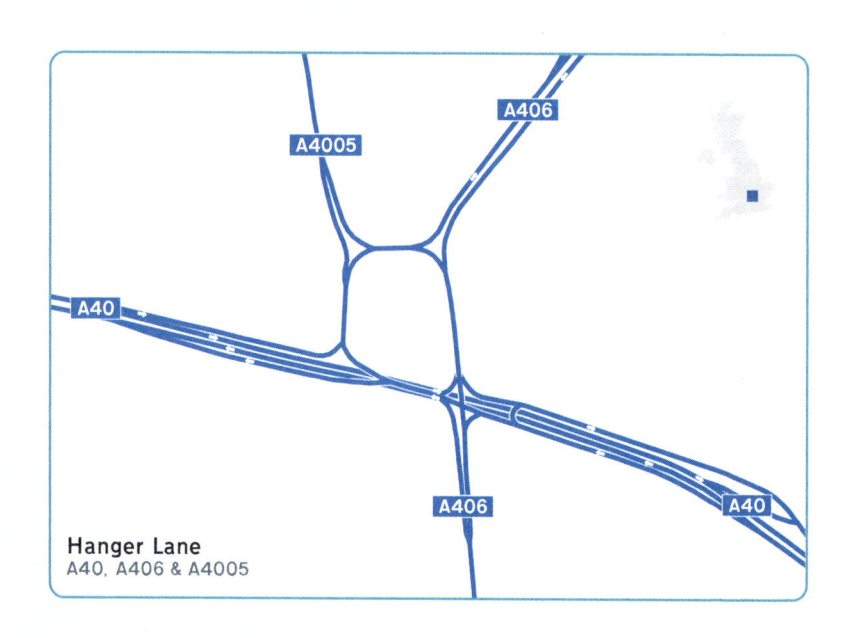

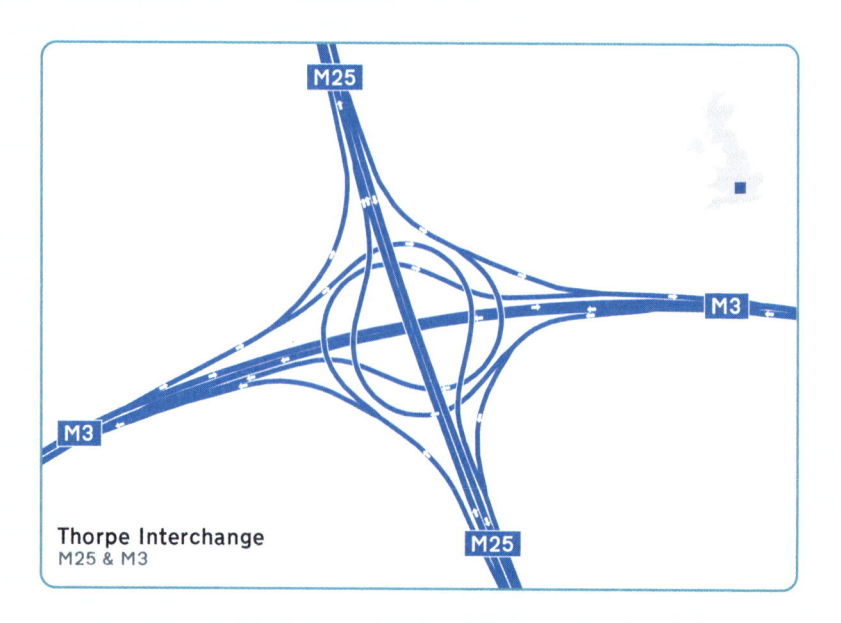

Thorpe Interchange
M25 & M3

Theydon Bois Interchange
M25 & M11

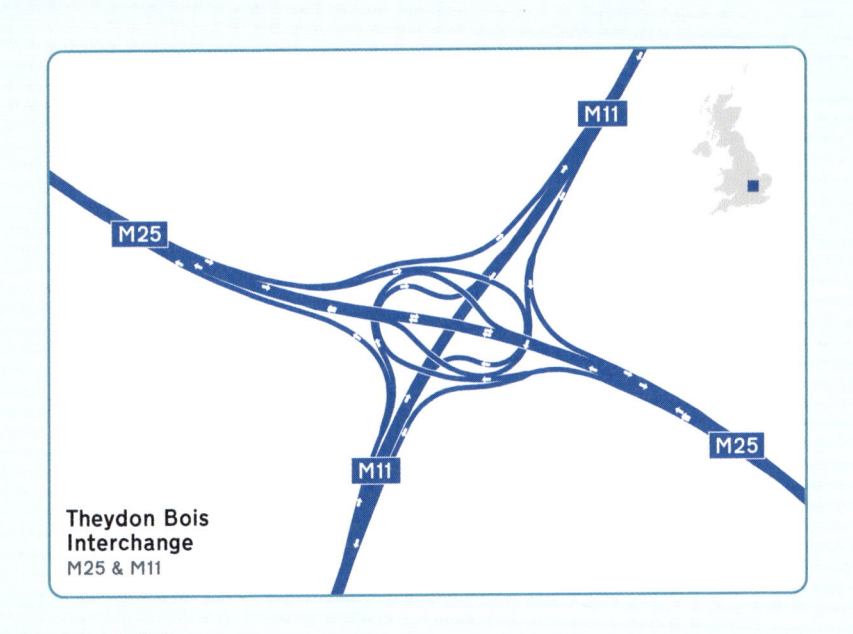

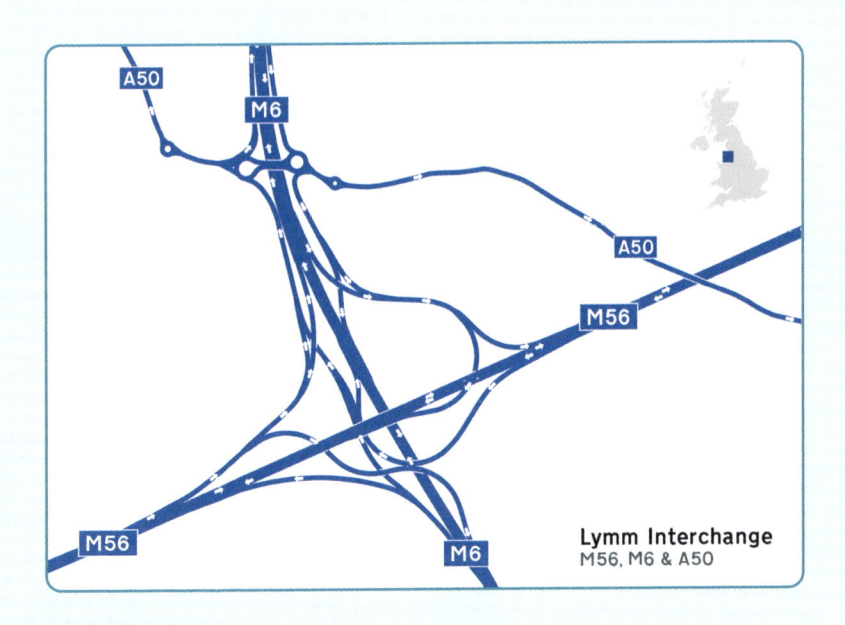

Lymm Interchange
M56, M6 & A50

Shipping lanes

Have you ever sat looking out at the ocean, and wondered why all of the ships appear to be following each other? It's not a trick of the eye – they really are! Just like cars and aeroplanes, ships typically follow pre-defined shipping lanes. Established during the 19th century, these navigable routes were designated to maximise efficiency and safety in narrow, busy channels. You can see how ships follow these lanes on this map of shipping density in and around UK waters.

The English Channel is by far the busiest section of water around the UK, with over 500 ships passing through it every day. The most congested area is the Dover Strait, the 23-mile (37-km) wide section of sea between Dover in Kent and Calais in France.

Another intensely busy region is the North Sea. With over 70 oil rigs, thousands of wind turbines and an estimated 6,600 active fishing vessels, it's a hive of industry – as well as being crucial for passenger and cargo transport around northern Europe.

As well as being necessary for commercial and safety reasons, some shipping lanes were developed to limit nautical activity across the UK's 377 Marine Protected Areas – which actually cover 38 per cent of British seas. This aims to reduce pollution and minimise disturbance of wildlife.

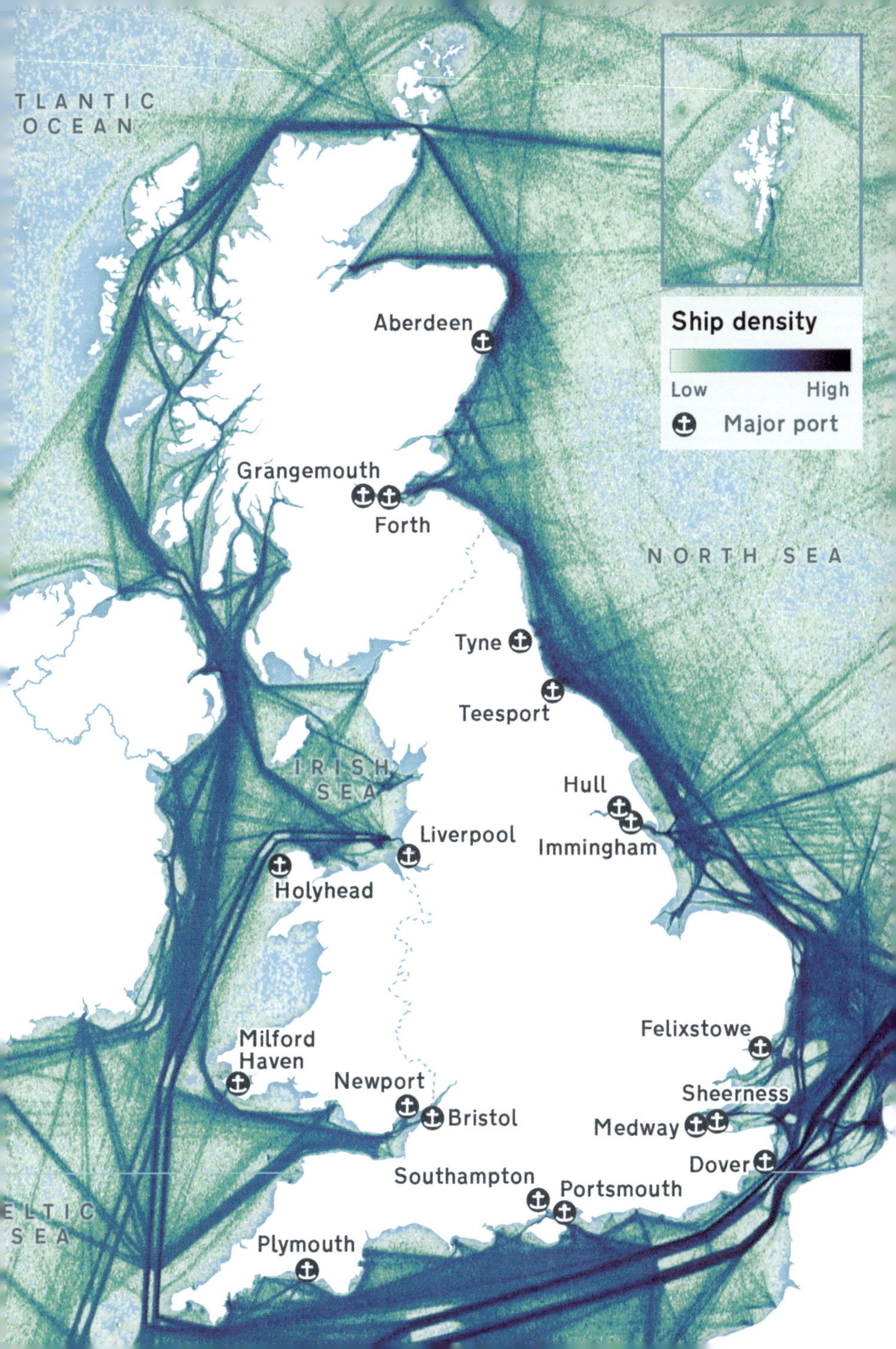

TLANTIC
OCEAN
Ship density
Low
High
Major port
Aberdeen
Grangemouth
Forth
NORTH SEA
Tyne
Teesport
IRISH
SEA
Hull
Immingham
Liverpool
Holyhead
Milford
Haven
Newport
Bristol
Felixstowe
Sheerness
Medway
Dover
Southampton
Portsmouth
ELTIC
SEA
Plymouth

Shipping Forecast locations

The Shipping Forecast is a mainstay of British radio, having been broadcast multiple times a day for over 150 years. While it was originally transmitted from 1861 via telegraph, its first radio broadcast was on New Year's Day, 1924 – where it has remained ever since.

Forecasts are given for the 31 'sea areas' – which you can see on the map here. The forecast includes information on wind direction and force, weather conditions, visibility and atmospheric pressure. Listeners can tune in four times a day – at 5am, 11am, 5pm and 11pm – for round-the-clock weather alerts, or just to help them sleep. In fact, the Shipping Forecast has become so popular with insomniacs that the BBC now produces a podcast called 'The Sleeping Forecast', which combines forecasts with classic music.

Just in case this isn't enough for listeners, they can also tune into the atmospherically named High Seas Forecast twice a day – at 9:30am and 9:30pm – to listen to predictions on wind direction and force, weather, visibility and storm warnings.

#	Area	#	Area
1	Viking	17	Biscay
2	North Utsire	18	Trafalgar
3	South Utsire	19	FitzRoy
4	Forties	20	Sole
5	Cromarty	21	Lundy
6	Forth	22	Fastnet
7	Tyne	23	Irish Sea
8	Dogger	24	Shannon
9	Fisher	25	Rockall
10	German Bight	26	Malin
11	Humber	27	Hebrides
12	Thames	28	Bailey
13	Dover	29	Fair Isle
14	Wight	30	Faroes
15	Portland	31	Southeast Iceland
16	Plymouth		

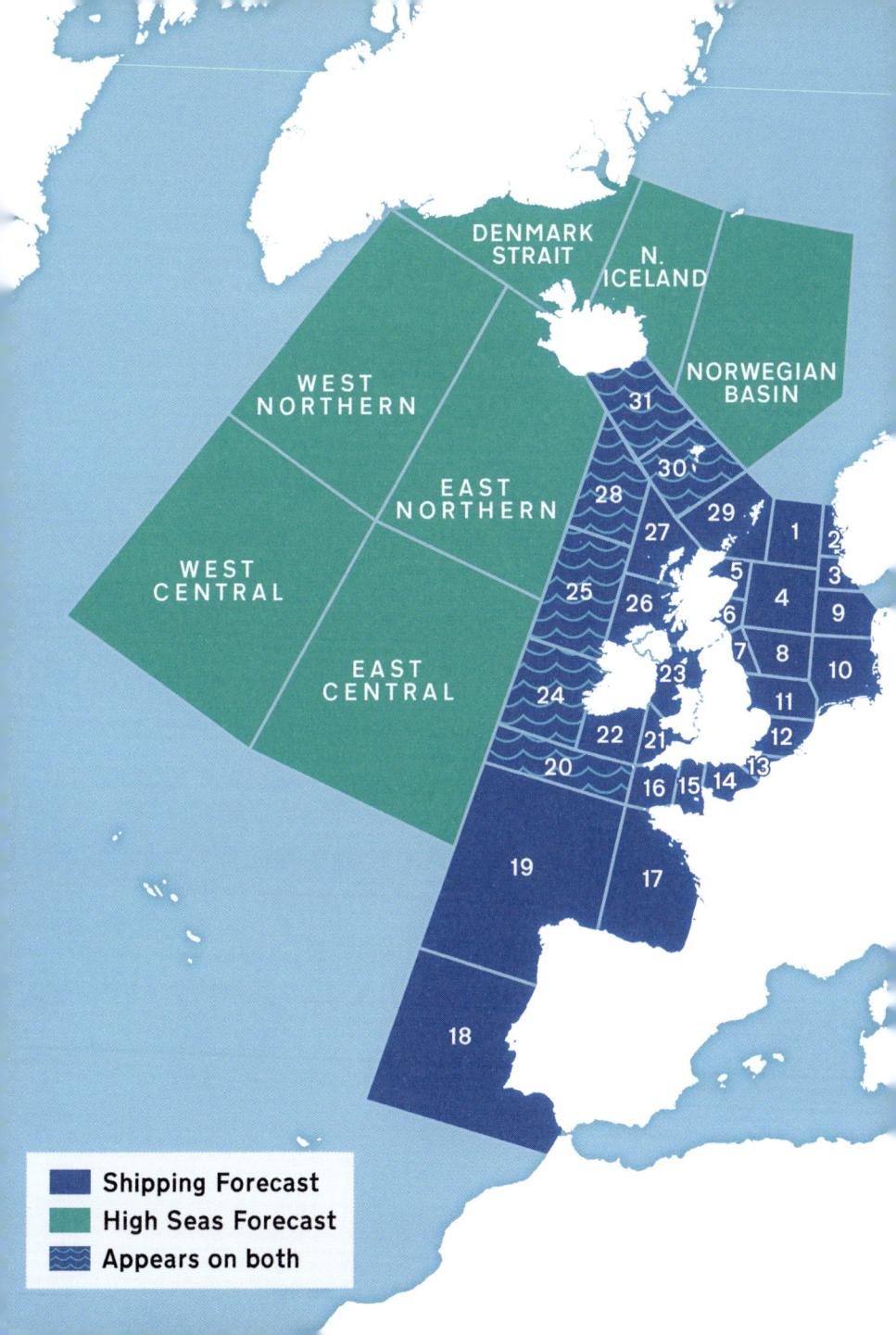

Map of Shipping Forecast and High Seas Forecast Areas

High Seas Forecast areas:
- DENMARK STRAIT
- N. ICELAND
- NORWEGIAN BASIN
- WEST NORTHERN
- EAST NORTHERN
- WEST CENTRAL
- EAST CENTRAL

Numbered areas (Shipping Forecast / Appears on both): 1–31

Legend:
- Shipping Forecast
- High Seas Forecast
- Appears on both

Lifestyle & Hobbies

From trainspotting to morris dancing – mapping Britain's most whimsical pastimes

Morris dancing teams

Is there a sight more British than a troupe of morris dancers cavorting in a pub garden on a warm summer's day? The waving of the handkerchiefs, the jingling of bells, the sheer determination to uphold one of the country's more eccentric traditions …

While morris dancing may seem like a remnant of a bygone era – it is thought to originate in the 15th century – the practice is alive and well. Around 740 troupes are active, with approximately 12,600 active members, according to the UK Morris Census (yes, there is a UK Morris Census). While traditionally morris dancing may be thought of as a pursuit for men, 2023 was actually the first year that more women dancers were recorded than men. Women-only morris dancing is sometimes referred to as 'carnival' or 'fluffy morris', which sounds like something you might see in a book about moths.

Morris dancing is particularly popular across England and Wales, and it's Yorkshire that takes the prize for the greatest number of morris dancing troupes, with around 80 currently operating.

The Cotswold style is the most popular. Despite the name, this type is danced across the whole of the UK, and is particularly dominant in southern England. This is the 'quintessential' morris style, and is danced with hankies and sticks, with dancers adorned in ribbons decorating their hats and waistcoats.

Beyond the common forms – such as Cotswold, Border and Rapper – some alternative modern twists on morris dancing have emerged. Take the Essex Hells Bells Morris, for example, who fuse Border Morris with steampunk, or Dartford's Screaming Banshees Gothic Morris – who perform exactly as the name suggests.

Number of teams

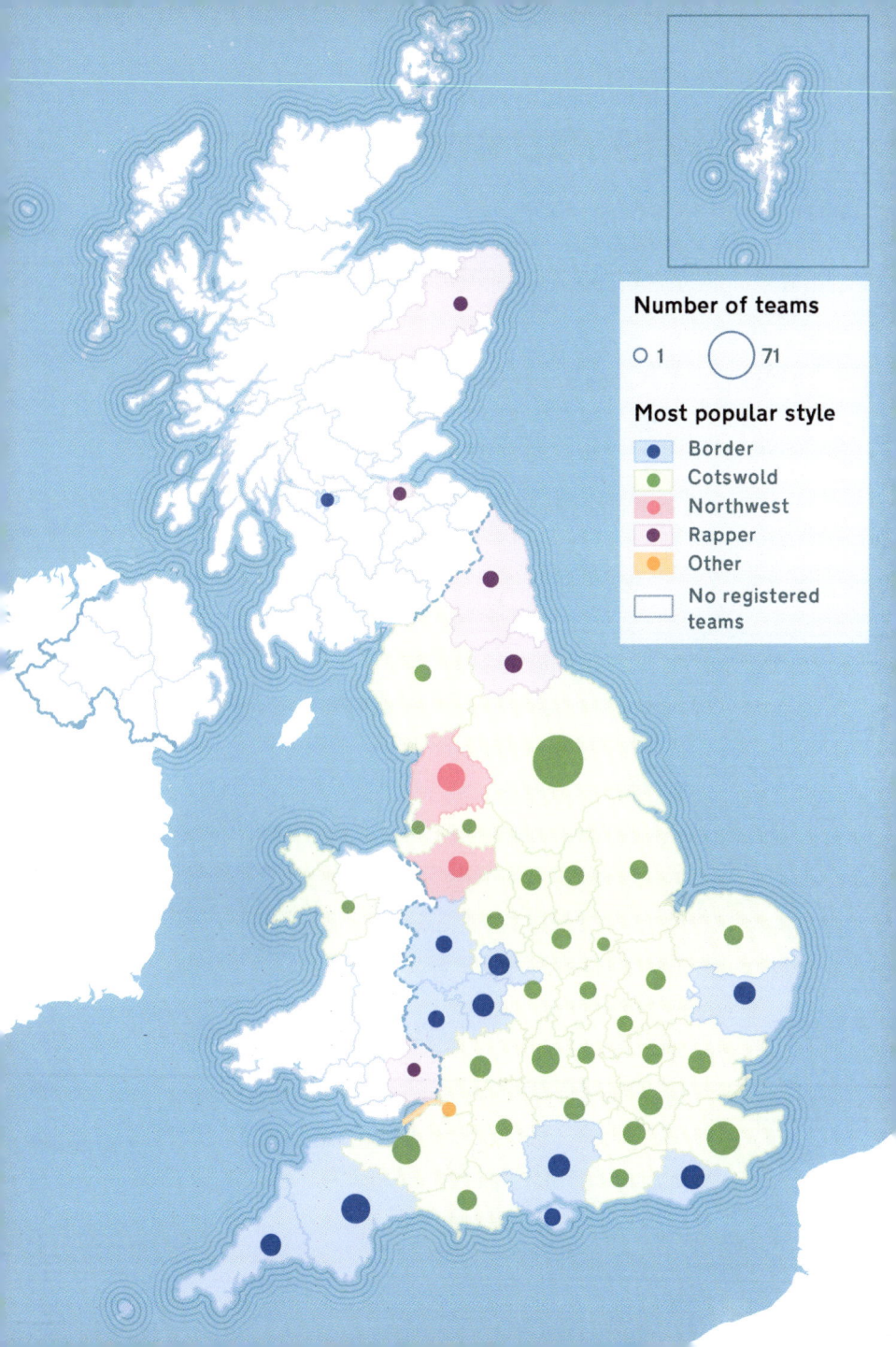

○ 1   ◯ 71

Most popular style

- Border
- Cotswold
- Northwest
- Rapper
- Other
- No registered teams

Quirkiest sports

The UK's favourite sport is – no surprises – football, with more than 55 million of us going to watch a match in 2023. As well as being home to the internationally beloved sports of football, rugby and cricket, the UK boasts a huge variety of unconventional local sports.

So, if you're tired of waiting for it to come home (any year now!), or you just prefer your sporting endeavours a little more on the quirky side, here are some of the UK's wackiest local pastimes.

There's something for everyone; whether you want to race a train, carry a wife or flonk a dwile (translation: fling a beer-soaked cloth at a circle of dancers). If it exists, we've probably turned it into a sport.

Some of these have achieved fame on the global stage. People flock from around the world to watch and participate in Gloucestershire's 'officially banned' cheese rolling. Llanwrtyd Wells' bog snorkeling championship is similarly renowned and has even been featured on Lonely Planet's 50 'must-do' experiences.

What do all of these sports have in common? They all take a love of the British everyday – from Yorkshire puddings to mud – and have turned them into a joyful pastime. Oh, and 90 per cent of them seem to have been invented in the pub.

- Quirky sport location

- Winter Swimming Championships
- World Stone Skimming Competition
- Haggis Hurling World Championships
- World Gurning Championships
- Yorkshire Pudding Boat Race
- World Gravy Wrestling Competition
- Welly Wanging
- World Egg Throwing Championships
- World Worm Charming Championships
- Toe Wrestling World Championships
- Dwile Flonking
- Race the Train
- Bog Snorkling
- Man v Horse
- Cheese Rolling
- Shin Kicking
- Wife Carrying Race
- Maldon Mud Race
- World Marble Championship
- Cornish Hurling
- Dorset Knob Throwing
- Lawn Mower Racing

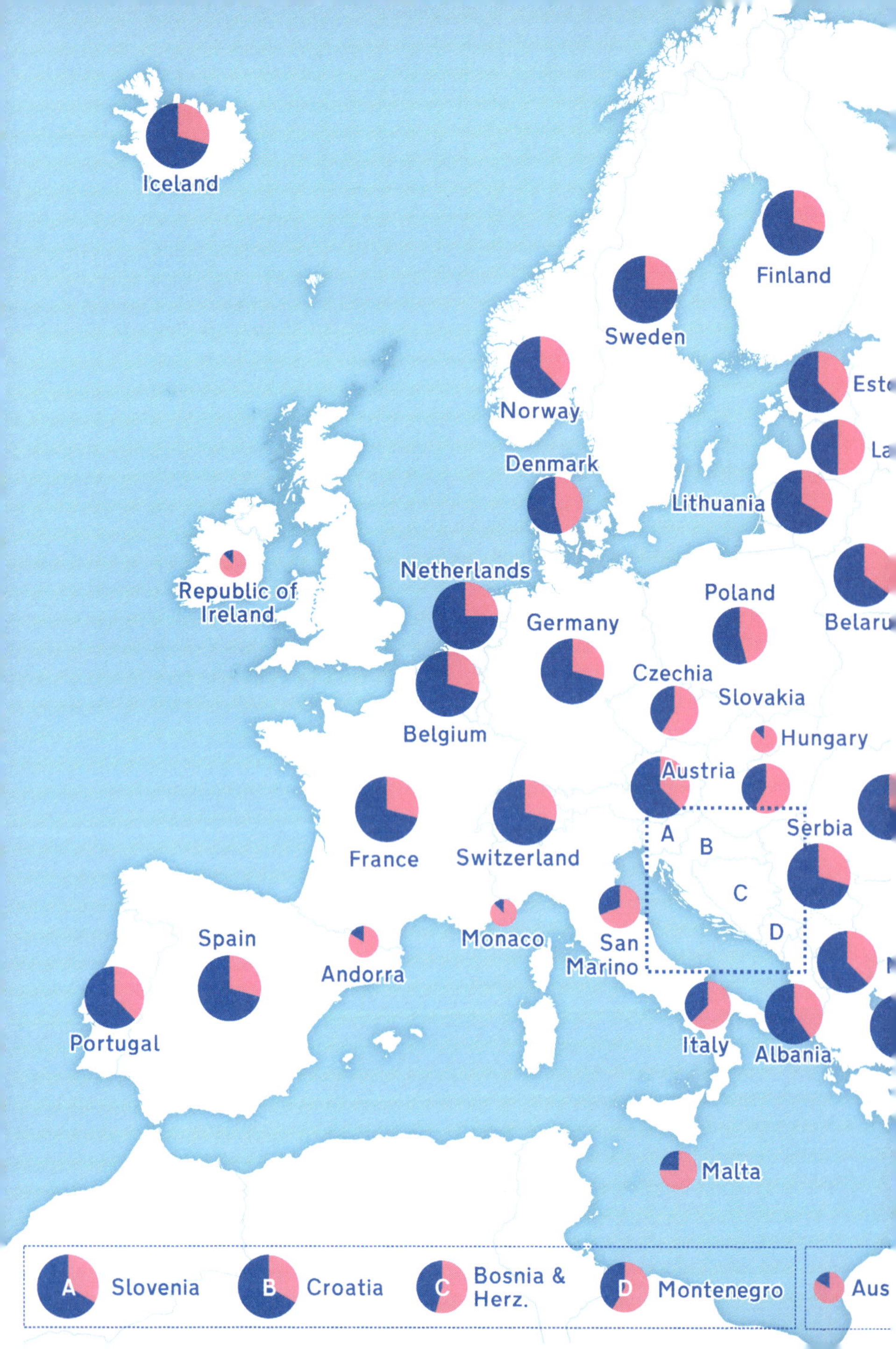

Iceland
Finland
Sweden
Norway
Esto
La
Denmark
Lithuania
Republic of Ireland
Netherlands
Poland
Belaru
Germany
Czechia
Slovakia
Belgium
Hungary
Austria
Serbia
A
B
C
D
France
Switzerland
Monaco
San Marino
Spain
Andorra
Portugal
Italy
Albania
Malta
A Slovenia
B Croatia
C Bosnia & Herz.
D Montenegro
Aus

Eurovision 'nul points'

Every year, there are two words which fill Brits with a sense of mingled shame and hilarity: 'nul points'. Britain is so famed for receiving no points in the Eurovision Song Contest that it was famously mocked for this in the 2020 film of the same name ... but how deserved is this reputation? Well ... very. Despite occasional shining moments of glory (Buck's Fizz, Katrina and the Waves, Sam Ryder and ... are there any others?), we really do not fare well in Eurovision. Since 2020, we've received 'nul points' from voting countries a whopping 907 times! Countries who particularly don't care for our musical stylings include Moldova, Azerbaijan, Serbia and the Netherlands – all of whom have awarded us zero points in over 75 per cent of contests. Our biggest allies? The Republic of Ireland, Monaco, Slovakia, as well as the not-so-European nation of Australia, have given us at least some points in 87.5 per cent of contests.

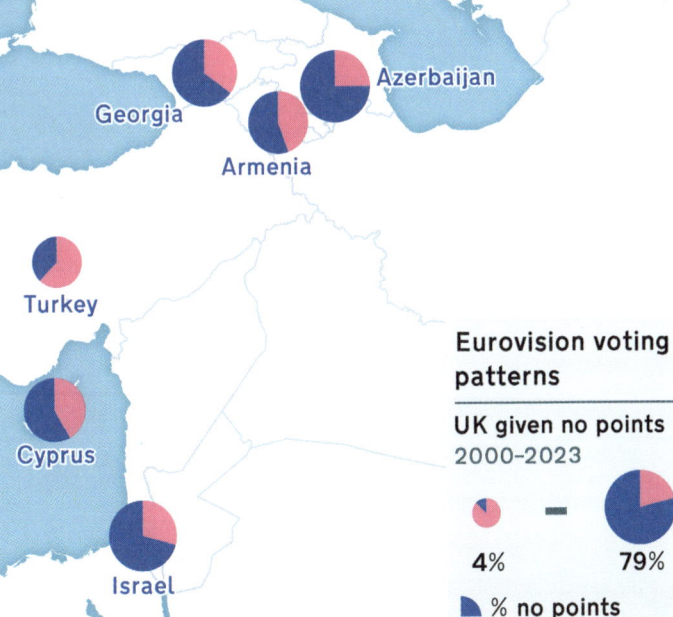

Eurovision voting patterns

UK given no points
2000–2023

4% — 79%

- % no points
- % some points

Top trainspotting locations
Rail network
Inverness Station
Glenfinnan Viaduct
Rannoch Station
Crianlarich Station
Forth Bridge
Bo'ness Station
Dunbar Station
Castlerock Beach
Botanic Station
Goathland Station
Skelton Tower
Colton Junction
Manchester Piccadilly
Llangollen Railway
Barnetby Station
Doncaster Station
Ffestiniog Railway
Crewe Station
Tamworth Station
Water Orton Station
Nuneaton Station
Lickey Incline
Ebury Bridge
Clapham Junction
Woody Bay Station

Top trainspotting sites

Did you know there are an estimated 100,000 trainspotters in the UK? These rail enthusiasts chase the ultimate goal of seeing EVERY train the UK has to offer, but with around 9,800 miles (15,800km) of track to cover, that's no easy task. So, if you're looking to complete trainspotting bingo, here are some of the top spots to visit.

Some of these feature on the map because of the sheer number of trains that can be seen from them. For example, Clapham Junction (or 'Clappers' as it's known – with varying degrees of affection – by locals), is the UK's busiest interchange station and sees a whopping 2,000 trains passing through every single day. Further north, Crewe Station is a key trainspotting sight, acting as a major junction connecting the strategic West Coast Main Line to other national and regional routes. Crewe is also one of the oldest stations in the world, having opened in 1837. With a heritage centre featuring a wide range of historic locomotives, it's a must-see destination for trainspotting aficionados.

Other hotspots on this map feature because of their breathtaking scenery. The award for the most famous scenic rail location in the UK has to go to Glenfinnan Viaduct, which can be found on the West Highland Line in Inverness-shire. Completed in 1901, perhaps its biggest claim to fame in recent years is its appearance in the *Harry Potter* films. Now trainspotters from around the world gather to catch the moment that a Jacobite steam train passes along it – maybe to Hogwarts, but probably just to Fort William.

Then there's Lickey Incline in the West Midlands, notable for being the steepest sustained main-line railway incline (1.52 degrees over 2 miles/3.2km) but also for just having such a fantastic name that it warrants a whole paragraph all to itself.

Garden centre density

It's official: the UK is crazy about gardening. The UK garden centre market is one of the biggest in the world, cashing in around £5 billion annually across roughly 2,000 garden centres.

Garden centre distribution roughly follows the geographic pattern you might expect. There are generally fewer per 100,000 residents in counties that are more urban – like Greater London, Manchester, Birmingham and Bristol. The highest rate of garden centres is in Rutland, where there are 19 centres per 100,000 people.

It's no surprise that there are so many garden centres across the UK. Around 42 per cent of the British population cite gardening as a hobby according to a survey by Lakeland, with the average Brit spending around two hours a week exercising their green fingers.

Gardening isn't just for people with traditional gardens. There has been a boom in 'small-space' gardening in recent years, and a rise in the popularity of 'vertical gardening', with plant pots being appended to walls, fences and ladders, to maximise space. Travel through any urban area and you'll see plants bursting out of balconies, rooftops, and even adorning windowsills.

Part of this boom comes from an increased knowledge of the physical and mental benefits of being around plants. They improve air quality, reduce stress, increase our productivity and trigger the release of serotonin – the happy hormone.

Garden centres
Number per 100,000 residents

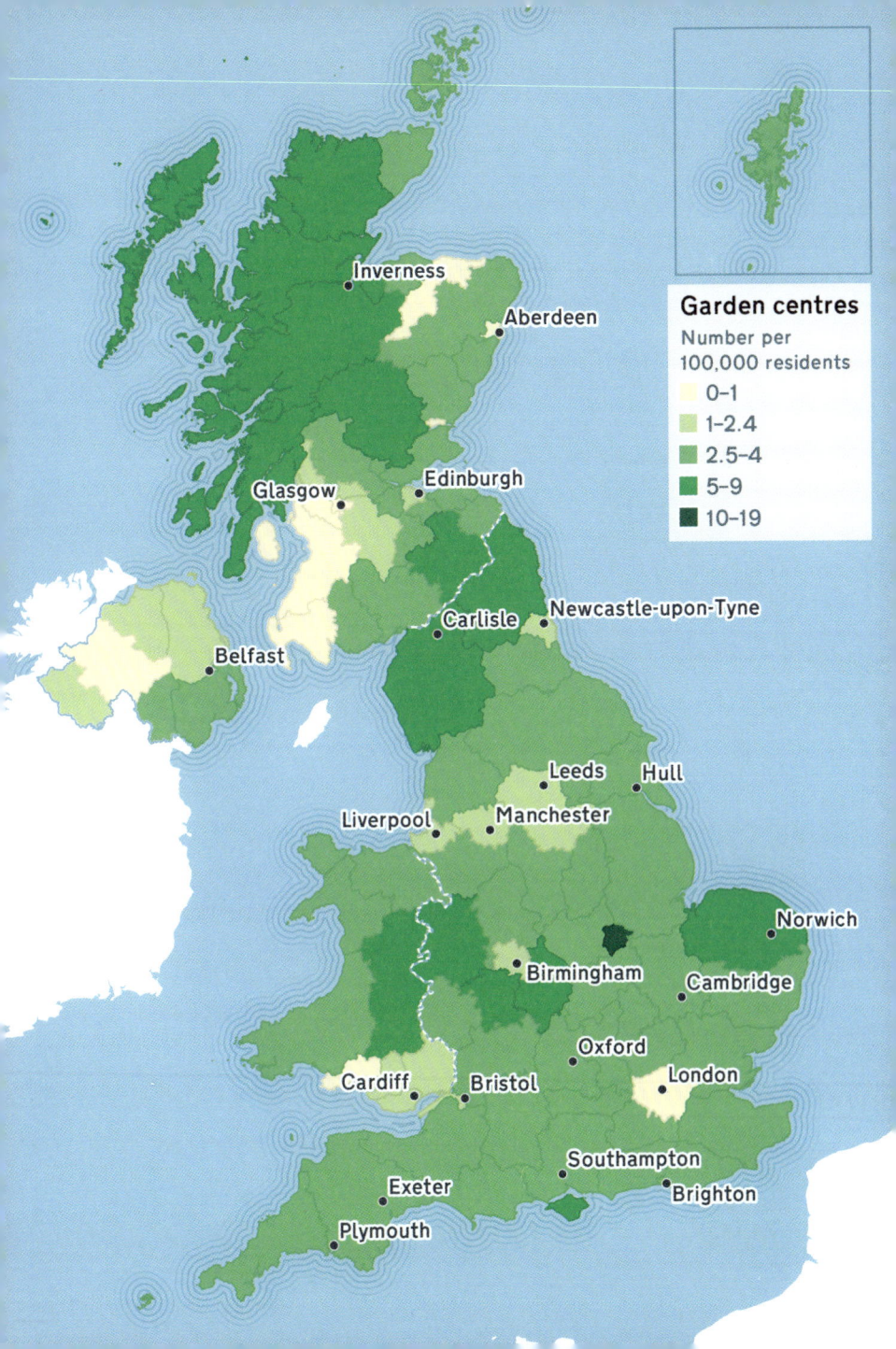

- 0–1
- 1–2.4
- 2.5–4
- 5–9
- 10–19

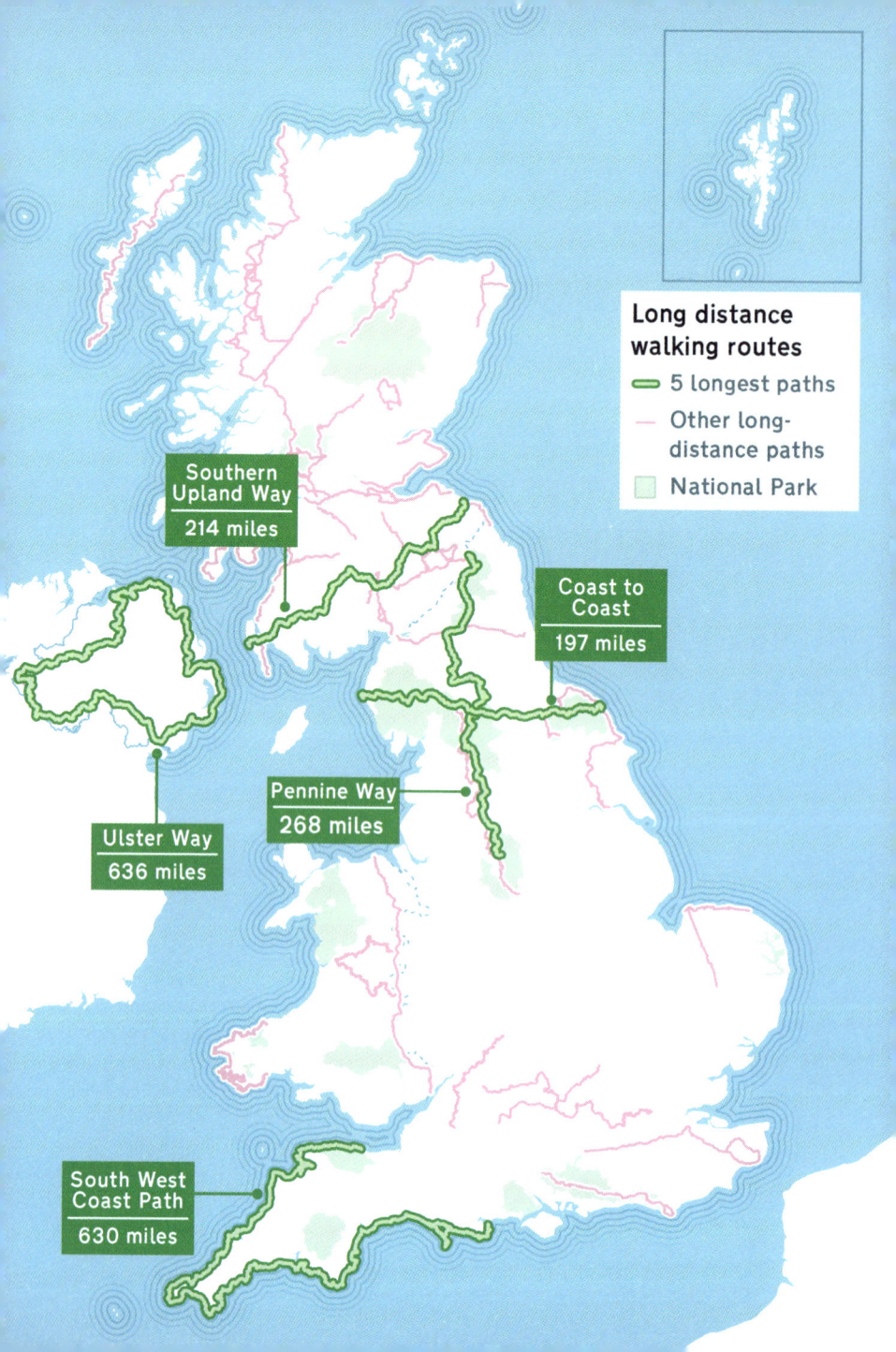

Long distance walking routes

- 5 longest paths
- Other long-distance paths
- National Park

Southern Upland Way — 214 miles

Coast to Coast — 197 miles

Ulster Way — 636 miles

Pennine Way — 268 miles

South West Coast Path — 630 miles

Longest walking routes

Whether it's a brisk 6am march around the local park, or a gruelling weekend hike, there's nothing quite like a walk to clear the mind and get the heart pumping. Luckily, the UK has no shortage of walking adventures, from short jaunts to very, very long-distance paths – the longest of which you can explore over the next couple of pages.

In 1965, the first National Trail – the Pennine Way – was established. This challenging path takes hikers 268 miles (431km) from Edale in Derbyshire to Kirk Yetholm in the Scottish Borders, traversing the Peak District and Yorkshire Dales along the way.

While Scotland and Northern Ireland do not have official national trails, the hikes available in these regions are no less stunning. In Northern Ireland, the longest waymarked trail (and in fact the longest trail in the whole of the UK) is the Ulster Way. Encircling most of the country, the trail covers an enormous 636 miles (1,024km) of beautiful Irish countryside. Scotland hosts 29 Great Trails which together stretch over 2,500 miles (4,000km). The longest of these is the Southern Upland Way that covers 214 miles (344km) across southern Scotland. However, the most popular route in the UK is the West Highland Way, running from Milngavie to Fort William. It's estimated that around 120,000 people use this trail each year – with around 36,000 completing the whole thing.

Far from being a historic designation, long-distance walking paths are being created all the time. The most recent National Trail – the Coast to Coast path – was designated in 2022. There is ongoing work to create a continuous English coast path (King Charles III England Coast Path), which will be the longest coastal path in the world!

Portstewart
Ballycastle
Coleraine
Ballymoney
Derry /
Londonderry
County
Derry /
Londonderry
Strabane
Ballymena
Magherafelt
Castlederg
County
Antrim
Cookstown
Omagh
County
Tyrone
Belfast
Bangor
Irvinestown
Dungannon
Craigavon
Enniskillen
Armagh
County
Down
County
Fermanagh
Downpatrick
Newry
County
Armagh
0
10
20 mi
Ulster Way
Route
10 mile marker

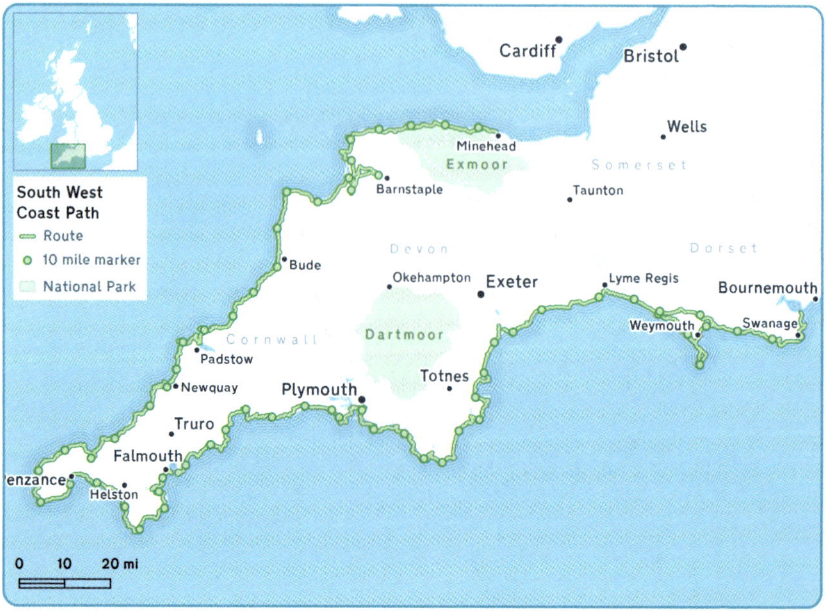
South West
Coast Path
Route
10 mile marker
National Park
Cardiff
Bristol
Wells
Minehead
Exmoor
Somerset
Barnstaple
Taunton
Devon
Dorset
Bude
Okehampton
Exeter
Lyme Regis
Bournemouth
Weymouth
Swanage
Cornwall
Dartmoor
Padstow
Totnes
Newquay
Plymouth
Truro
Falmouth
enzance
Helston
0
10
20 mi

Loch Lomond and The Trossachs

Glasgow
Edinburgh
Ayr

Southern Upland Way

Northumberland

Newcastle-upon-Tyne

Carlisle
Durham
Middlesbrough

Coast to Coast

Lake District
Yorkshire Dales
North York Moors

Lancaster
York
Hull
Leeds

Pennine Way

Manchester
Liverpool
Sheffield
Lincoln

Bangor
Peak District
Nottingham

Wolverhampton

Route
10 mile marker

0 20 40 mi

Index

Aberdeen 72, 107
Abernethy Biscuit 58
Anglo-Saxons 46
Argyll and Bute 92

Baked Bean Museum of Excellence 40
baked goods, regional 58–9
barn owls 77
Barrow Gurney 13
Barry 13
BBC 114
beaches 90–1
Belfast 58
Betty Mundy's Bottom 10
Big Garden Birdwatch 78
birds 76–9
Birmingham 102, 126
Bishop's Itchington 8
blackbirds 77
Blackwater Reservoir 96
Blickling Hall 36
blue tits 78
Bodiam Castle 31
Boleyn, Anne 36
Boscastle 40
bottoms (place names) 8, 10–11
bread 46–7
Brecon Beacons Dark Sky Reserve 26
Bristol 70, 102, 104, 126
British Isles, definition 5
Britons 14
Broadstairs, Kent 34
Brownsea Island 72
Bryn Eglwys quarries 39
Buck's Fizz 123

Caernarfon Castle 31
Cairn Gorm 95
Cairn Terriers 68
Caithness and Sutherland 25
Calais 19, 34, 112
Cardiff 70
castles 30–1, 36
cattle 80–1, 83
Channel Islands 5
cheese rolling 120
Chelsea Buns 58
Chepstow Castle 31
Chew Magna 13
Chillingham Castle 36
Chilterns 10
Christchurches 19
Christianity 49
Christmas 77, 96–7
cities 25
Clapham Junction 125
Clumber Spaniels 68
Coast to Coast path 129
Cocker Spaniels 68

Conwy Castle 31
Corfe Castle 36
Corgis 68
Cornish pasties 56–7
Cornwall 14, 31, 34, 40, 52, 56–7, 63, 91
Corrour Station 25
Cotswolds 43
Crackpot 8
Cretaceous period 70
Crewe Junction 125
cricket 120
crisp flavours 50–1
Crystal Palace, London 68
Cucumber Corner 8

Dachshunds 68
Dalegarth 39
Danelaw 14
Dark Sky Parks 26–7
Dartmoor 39
David I 31
DEFRA 81
Derwent Valley 74
Devon 39, 57, 63, 91
dinosaurs 70–1
dog breeds 68–9
Doggerland 67
Doncaster 13
'Doom Bar, the' 34
Dorset 19, 36, 70, 72
Dover 19, 112
Dover Strait 112
Doyden Castle 31
Droop 8
Dull 8
Dundee City 107
Dunseverick Castle 31

Edale 129
Edinburgh 31, 102
Edward I 31
Elizabeth II 63
England 5, 32, 60, 72, 102, 118
English Channel 112
English Civil War 36
Essex Hells Bells Morris 118
Eurovision Song Contest 122–3
Exeter 102

farm animals 80–3
Fifteens 58
fish and chips 52–3, 54–5
fishing 112
Flamborough Head 70
'flonk a dwile' 120
Flow Country 25
food & drink 45–63
football 120
Formby Red Squirrel Reserve 72
Fort William 125, 129

fossils 70–1
Foula, Shetland Islands 25
Freemasonry 40
French Bulldogs 68

Galloway Forest Dark Sky Park 26
garden centres 126–7
George Inn, Norton St Philip 43
Glasgow 31, 72, 102
Glenfinnan Viaduct 125
goats 82–3
Golden Retrievers 68
Gordon Setters 68
Great Trails 129
Great Yarmouth 56, 102
grey squirrels 72
Gulf Stream 88

Hampton Court 36
Harry Potter films 125
Haudagain Roundabout 107
haunted sites 36–7
Headhunters Barber Shop and Railway Museum 40
Henry VII 49
Henry VIII 36, 56
heritage 29–43
Hever Castle 36
High Seas Forecast 114–15
Highlands 25, 88, 95, 96
history 14–17, 29–43
hobbies 117–31
Hose 8

Ianstown 8
Inverie 25
Ipswich 34
Ireland 5, 123
Irish Tattie Bread 58
Isle of Man 5
Isle of Skye 70
Isle of Wight 20, 22, 70, 72

James II of England 43
James II of Scotland 74
John, King 56
Julian calendar 25
Jump 8
Jurassic Coast 70

Katrina and the Waves 123
Keith 8
Kennel Club, The 68
Kielder Forest Stargazing 26
Kirk Yetholm 129

Labrador Retrievers 68
Lake District 25, 39, 72, 95, 96
Lakeland 126
Land's End 91
Leicester 13

Lichfield 13
Lickey Incline 125
lifestyle 117–31
light pollution 26–7
lighthouses 20–1
Lindo, David 77
Liverpool 34
Lizard Peninsula 34, 91
Lizard Point 20
Llanwrtyd Wells' bog snorkeling championship 120
London 52, 74, 77, 88, 102, 126
Loose Bottom 10
Lyme Regis 70

M3 Thorpe Interchange 108
M24 108
M25 108
Magic Roundabout 107
Manchester 52, 77, 126
Marconi, Guglielmo 20
Marine Protected Areas 112
Mayon 52
Met Office 96
microclimates 88–9
Milngavie 129
Milton Keynes 107
Moffat Dark Sky community 26
Monmouth Rebellion 43
morris dancing 118–19
motorways 102–3
Museum of Witchcraft and Magic 40
museums, quirky 40–1

National Trails 129
National Trust properties 32–3
National Trust for Scotland 32
nature 65–83
Needles Lighthouse 20
New Forest 10
Newcastle 74
Normans 14, 31, 46
North Sea 26, 112
Northern Ireland 5, 32, 58, 60, 72, 78, 83, 92, 95, 102, 129
Northumberland Dark Sky Park 26

oak 67
oats 58
oil rigs 112
Old English 10, 14
Old Ferry Boat pub, St Ives 43
Old Forge pub, Inverie 25
Old Norse 14
Orkney 20
Outer Hebrides 77, 88, 95, 97
Oxford 7

Padstow 91
Pangea 70
Peak District 10, 129
Pennine Way 129
Pennines 95, 96
Perseid Meteor Shower 26
Peterborough 70

piers 22–3
pigs 81, 83
Pity Me 8
place 7–25
place names, weird 8–9
Pontefract 13
population density 24–5
Porch House pub 43
poultry 81–2, 83
Publow 13
pubs, oldest 42–3

race the train 120
rainiest places 92–3
Ramsbottom 10
Ravenglass and Eskdale Railway 39
red kites 74–5
red squirrels 72–3
Richard III 13
Ring of Iron 31
road junctions, complex 108–11
road names, strange 104–5
roast dinners 48–9
robins 76–7
Romans 14
roundabout hubs 106–7
Roxburgh Castle 31
Royal Society for the Protection of Birds (RSPB) 74, 78
rugby 120
Rutland 126
Ryder, Sam 123

St Catherine's Oratory 20
St Helen's, Lundy Island 25
Salford 13
Saxons 14
Scafell Pike 39
Scone (village) 60
scones 62–3, 60–1
Scotland 5, 25, 31, 58, 60, 67, 68, 72, 78, 82, 92, 95, 96, 99, 102, 129
Scottish Borders 129
Scratchy Bottom 8
Screaming Banshees Gothic Morris 118
Scunthorpe 13
seagulls 77
Second World War 18
Sennen Cove 52
serotonin 126
Seymour, Jane 56
Shakespeare, William 74
sheep 81, 82
Shepherd and Flock Roundabout 107
Sherborne 19
Shetland Islands 20, 77, 88, 95, 97
Shetland Reestit Mutton Pie 58
Shipping Forecast 114–15
shipping lanes 112–13
shipwrecks 34–5
'shorts weather' 98–9
Skegness 13
Skirrid Inn 36

Smallest House museum 40
Smith, Frank 50
Solent 20
South Devon Railway 39
South Foreland Lighthouse 20
South West peninsula 88, 90–1
Southampton 34
Southend Pier 22
Southern Upland Way 129
Spaghetti Junction 108
Spanker Lane 104
sparrows 78
sports, quirky 120–1
Stirling Castle 31
Stow-on-the-Wold 43
sunshine 90–1
Swanage 70
Swansea 13
Swindon 107

Talyllyn Railway 39
Thames Estuary 34
Thorney Junction 108
Titty Ho 104
Tolkien, J. R. R. 104
Totnes 39
Tower of London 36
towns 12–13, 18–19
trains, steam 38–9
trainspotting 124–5
transport 101–15
trees, oldest 66–7
Triassic period 70
Tudors 36

Ulster Way 129
United Kingdom of Great Britain and Northern Ireland (UK) 5

Victorian era 22, 40, 68
Vikings 14

Wales 5, 25, 31, 32, 36, 39, 60, 68, 72, 74, 82, 95, 102, 118
walking routes, longest 128–31
Warley Museum 40
weather 85–99
Welsh Corgis 68
West Coast Main Line 125
West Highland Line 125
West Highland Way 129
Whip-Ma-Whop-Ma-Gate, York 104
Whitby 70
Wicca 40
wife-carrying 120
wind turbines 95, 112
windiest areas 94–5
Woodland Trust 72

yew, Fortingall 67
Yorkshire Dales 10, 96, 129

Acknowledgements

A huge thanks to the organizations who have provided the data which has made these maps possible.

Pages 10–11, 14–17, 30, 103, 107, 109–111, 127: © OpenStreetMap contributors data via the Open Database License.

Page 24: WorldPop (www.worldpop.org - School of Geography and Environmental Science, University of Southampton; Department of Geography and Geosciences, University of Louisville; Departement de Geographie, Universite de Namur) and Center for International Earth Science Information Network (CIESIN), Columbia University (2018). Global High Resolution Population Denominators Project - Funded by The Bill and Melinda Gates Foundation (OPP1134076). https://dx.doi.org/10.5258/SOTON/WP00674

Page 27: Annual VNL V2, C. D. Elvidge, M. Zhizhin, T. Ghosh, F-C. Hsu, "Annual time series of global VIIRS nighttime lights derived from monthly averages: 2012 to 2019", Remote Sensing (In press)

Pages 32–33: National Trust (2025) created by Dominic Beddow for sourcing this data.

Page 35: Shipwreck locations (2024) public sector information from the United Kingdom Admiralty Marine Data Solutions, licensed under the Open Government Licence v3.0.

Pages 38, 47, 48, 51, 54–55, 56–57, 59, 61, 62, 79, 80–83, 93, 98, 106, 119, 124, 127: Ordnance Survey data © Crown copyright and database rights [2025].

Pages 47, 48, 51, 54–55, 61, 62, 98: Utterly British Maps survey data (2025) created by Helen McKenzie.

Page 71: Paleobiology Database: Uhen, M.D., B. Allen, N. Behboudi, M. E. Clapham, E. Dunne, A. Hendy, P. A. Holroyd, M. Hopkins, P.Mannion, P. Novack-Gottshall, C. Pimiento, and P. Wagner. 2023. Paleobiology Database User Guide Version 1.0. PaleoBios 40(11): 1-56. paleobiodb.org

Page 73: Red Squirrel Occurrence NBN Trust (2024). The National Biodiversity Network (NBN) Atlas. https://ror.org/00mcxye41.

Page 73: Scottish Wildlife Trust (2019). The Scottish Squirrel Database.

Page 73: Natural Resources Wales (2020). Ty Canol National Nature Reserve (NNR) Species Inventory.

Page 73: COFNOD (2019). Mammal records captured from Licence Returns submitted to Natural Resources Wales (primarily mammal records).

Page 73: Natural Resources Wales (2020). Natural Resources Wales (NRW) Licence Return Dataset.

Page 73: Natural History Museum (2023). Data Portal query on 1 resources.

Page 73: Northern Ireland Environment Agency (NIEA) Collated Species Records, CEDaR (2019).

Page 73: Pamplin, F. (2019). Survey of Eurasian otter (Lutra lutra) distribution in the Glenmore - Aviemore area. Scottish Natural Heritage Report.

Page 73: Scottish Wildlife Trust (2019). Survey and monitoring records for Scottish Wildlife Trust reserves from reserve convenors and Trust volunteers - Verified data.

Page 73: Scottish Wildlife Trust (2019). Commissioned surveys and staff surveys and reports for Scottish Wildlife Trust reserves - Verified data.

Page 73: Mammal Society (2022). Mammal Mapper App Sighting Records.

Page 73: Natural Resources Wales (2019). NRW Regional Data: all taxa (excluding sensitive species), West Wales.

Page 73: Hsing, P.-Y., Hill, R. A., Smith, G. C., Bradley, S., Green, S. E., Kent, V. T., Mason, S. S., Rees, J., Whittingham, M. J., Cokill, J., MammalWeb citizen scientists & Stephens, P. A. (2022). Large-scale mammal monitoring: The potential of a citizen science camera-trapping project in the United Kingdom. Ecological Solutions and Evidence.

Page 73: Caledonian Conservation (2020). Caledonian Conservation Ltd Incidental Records 2014 onwards.

Pages 73, 75, 76: NBN Trust (2025). The National Biodiversity Network (NBN) Atlas. https://ror.org/00mcxye41.

Page 75: Royal Society for the Protection of Birds (2023). Records provided by Royal Society for the Protection of Birds, accessed through NBN Atlas website.

Page 75: Argyll Biological Records Centre (2023). Argyll Biological Records Dataset. Occurrence dataset on the NBN Atlas. DOI: 10.15468/ejve6c.

Page 75: Birda (2023). Records provided by Birda, accessed through NBN Atlas website.

Page 76: Royal Society for the Protection of Birds (2023). Records provided by Royal Society for the Protection of Birds, accessed through NBN Atlas website.

Page 76: Argyll Biological Records Centre (2023). Argyll Biological Records Dataset. Occurrence dataset on the NBN Atlas. DOI: 10.15468/ejve6c.

Page 76: Birda (2023). Records provided by Birda, accessed through NBN Atlas website.